MAYHEM!

More From the Master of Malice

George Hayduke

A Lyle Stuart Book
Published by Carol Publishing Group

CONTENTS

BY WAY OF
INTRODUCTION

In my last book, I made editorial hamburger out of a rude jock named Dave Kingman. This time I wish to pay honored homage to another retired baseball star, a clever young chap named Jay Johnstone. An excellent ball player with a great sense of humor and reality, Johnstone is a natural Hayduker. Many of his escapades are related in his book *Temporary Insanity*, a highly recommended read.

Johnstone makes a good point about two rules of Hayduking: revenge is a stew best served cold, and you don't wait around to get blamed for something you've just done. Johnstone writes:

> It was another triumph. By that time I was at the far end of the clubhouse, busy doing something else. Most guys want to be there to gloat....Not me....I won't even be in the neighborhood. It's always better when someone else gets blamed.

My mother, talk show hosts, and other worrying do-gooders are always asking me why I tell people ways to get revenge on their tormentors and other bullies. Besides being a bullybuster, my calling in life, I also feel my books and ideas help relieve stress in our mean-spirited world.

In the Hayduke lexicon, stress is the confusion created when your mind overrides your own self's basic desire to choke the living shit out of some asshole who desperately needs it. There is little sense in meeking it through until Earth-inheritance day. Or consider that if you make yourself into a sheep, you will soon meet a very hungry fox, which is an old Russian proverb as applicable today here in the land of the Great Satan as it was then in the land of the Imperial Queen.

We Americans say "Don't make waves," while our Sicilian friends use the old homily "Do not disturb the cattle," meaning about the same thing: Do not bother the cattle and they will provide you with rich, sweet cream and calm, tender beef. You may consider this a literal analogy for our collective, dumped-upon public. Do you like being bullied and shat upon? I don't and neither should you.

You have to stand up to these bullies and bust their chops. I don't mean that literally, as I prefer the more subtle approaches that bend minds rather than bodies; in the long term, that is much more effective. Of course, if you can do both, well, I, ahh, cough, cough...

This philosophy is a great deal like public opinion, and public opinion is like an elephant. If you prod it correctly, it will go where you wish, but until you are its master there is nothing much else that is powerful enough to stop it. So it is when dealing with bullies.

You can't be a wimp about this, someone who wouldn't go pop if he or she had a mouthful of firecrackers. Of course, in civilized times, a gentlemanly or ladylike understanding is fine, but I sometimes feel it is better to carry a large caliber pistol.

It all comes down to that one story told to the guys at the gun shop by the mighty hunter of people, games, toys, and fun times, my good pal, the nicely retired Donald C. Steffey, Gny. Sgt., USMC.

"One day when the Corps had me serving in Vietnam," the genial giant told his spellbound audience, "a tiger and a bull got into a terrible fight. After a tremendous struggle, the tiger killed the bull, then proceeded to eat the carcass.

"Filled and pleased with himself, this tiger threw back his head and let out a mighty roar. This roar attracted the attention of one of our kids on sentry, who promptly spotted the tiger and shot him dead on the spot.

"The moral of this story, guys, is when you are full of bull it's best to keep your mouth shut."

As yet another old vet stretching the seams of middle-aged girth, I can vouch for Gunny Steffey's advice. After all, you can only do so much—when the *Titanic* is sinking, it does little good to start bailing with a shot glass.

One of the best pieces of advice I offer new Haydukers is *not* to brag about what you're going to do or have done. Do your business without any fanfare. You want to be like that fellow who's wearing the blue wool suit and can't make it to the bathroom in time, so he pisses in his pants. He has this warm feeling, but nobody else knows what's going on. Learn to love anonymity.

Anonymity is such a wimp-word, of course. I much prefer the simple advice given by Andrew McGeary as he surveyed the site of the Roark's Drift battle of Zulu War fame with his father and uncles. Young Andrew said, "When we McGearys go on safari, the lions roll up their windows."

Animals usually have their shit together far better than we humans. After all, when the hungry owl drops in on the annual Mouse Day picnic, he has much more in mind than entering the sack race. As in all nature, there are anomalies...and I used to be one.

Freddie Sykes, my true identity in another life, once said that to truly get even with people for something hurtful they'd done to you, all you had to do was to "tear, then pull the scab off their foot slowly, very slowly, just beyond the point of where it stings." Old Freddie was talking figuratively, of course.

Yet as you begin your chortlingly personal journey through this book, I offer my own final thoughts on the matter. Armed with the information in *Mayhem!*, you can be sure your marks and markesses would rather run through a gauntlet of pit bulls wearing pork chop underwear than hassle you or me.

George Hayduke
La Matanza, Nicaragua

A SPECIAL REQUEST

I get a lot of mail, all of which I answer myself. Most of the mail is fun, some of it is bonkers, while some of it comes from people with the personality of stale vomit. I try to respond to everyone who writes. But, if you don't include some valid return address, even if it's a mail drop, I can't write back to you. Some great folks write to me with great ideas or with sincere questions, but they don't let me know where I am to send a response.

If you write to me and want me to respond personally, please give me a return address. Fair enough?

SOME PHILOSOPHIC ADVICE

I'm a bullybuster, here to help you exact revenge upon the pencil necks, jerks, geeks, institutions, corporations, bureaucrats, and other assorted assholes with black hearts or Styrofoam pellets for brains. I always practice the traditional Golden Rule, but sometimes have to substitute the Hayduke Rule: "Do unto others before they get unto you." I also recall some advice George B. Shaw gave someone. A classic curmudgeon, Shaw was always giving someone advice. He wrote, "Do not do unto others as you would that they should unto you. Their tastes may not be the same."

I recall back in high school when Dot Harpster had us read Shaw, I knew right then and there that here was a man I could admire. And I do.

GENERAL ADVICE

Throughout this book I make universal reference to the "mark," which is a street label hung on the victim, male or female, of a scam or con or act of vengeance. In our case, the mark is a bully—anyone or anything—who has done something unpleasant, foul, or unforgivable to you, your family, your property, or your friends. Never think of a mark as the victim of dirty tricks. Think of the mark as a very deserving bully, a target of your revenge.

Before you study any of the specific sections of this book, read these next few vital paragraphs. They tell you how to prepare before going into action.

1. Prepare a plan.

Plan all details before you take action at all. Don't even ad-lib something from this book without a plan of exactly what you're going to do and how. If your campaign involves a series of actions, make a chronological chart (don't forget to destroy it when you're through), and then coordinate your efforts. Make a list of possible problems. Plan what you'll do if you get caught—depending upon who catches you. You must have every option, contingency, action, reaction, and evaluation planned in advance. Remember, time is usually on the side of the trickster. As Winston Churchill—who is one of my favorite heroes for many, many reasons—once said, "A lie gets halfway around the world before the truth even puts on its boots." Or, as that old Sicilian homily goes, "Revenge is a dish best served cold," which means don't strike while your ire is hot. Wait. Plan. Think. Learn.

2. Gather intelligence.

Do what a real intelligence operative would do and compile a file on your mark. How detailed and thorough you are depends upon your plans for the mark. For a simple get-even number, you obviously need less inside information than if you're planning an involved, time-release campaign. Before you start spying, make a written list of all the important things you need to know about the target—be it a person, company, or institution.

3. Buy away from home.

Any supplies, materials, or services you need must be purchased away from where you live. Buy far in advance and pay in cash. Try to be as inconspicuous and colorless as possible. Don't talk unnecessarily with people. The best rule here is the spy's favorite—a good operative will get lost in a crowd of one. The idea is for people not to remember you.

4. Never tip your hand.

Don't get cocky, cute 'n clever, and start dropping hints about who's doing what to whom. I know that may sound stupid, but some would-be tricksters *are* gabby. Of course, in some of the cases this will not apply, e.g., unselling car customers at the dealership, or other tricks in which the scenario demands your personal involvement.

5. Never admit anything.

If accused, act shocked, hurt, outraged, or amused, whichever seems appropriate. Deny everything, unless, again, your plan involves overt personal involvement. If you're working covert, stay that way. The only cool guy out of Watergate was G. Gordon Liddy; he kept his mouth shut.

6. Never apologize; it's a sign of weakness.

Normally, harassment of a citizen is a low-priority case with the police. The priority increases along with the mark's socioeconomic status in the community and with his or her political connections. If you are at war with a corporation, utility, or institution, that's a different ball game. They often have private security people, sometimes retired federal or state investigators. By habit, these people may not play according to the law. If you play dirty tricks upon a governmental body, prepare to have a case opened. But how hard it is followed depends upon a lot of factors. Understanding all this ahead of time is part of your intelligence planning before you get started.

THE ELEVEN COMMANDMENTS OF REVENGE

Thanks to my Apostle of Revenge, Dick Smegma, I humbly present for your perusal, belief, and adherence, the Eleven Commandments of Revenge. Stay faithful and you'll enjoy a lot of yucks without suffering the heartbreak of being caught.

1. *Thou shalt neither trust nor confide in anyone!*
   If you do, that person could eventually betray you. Even if it is a relative or spouse, don't tell anybody what you are up to. Implicated accomplices are OK.
2. *Thou shalt never use thy own telephone for revenge business!*
   Always use a public telephone or that of an unwitting mark so calls cannot be traced back to you or to someone who knows you.
3. *Thou shalt not touch revenge documents with thy bare hands!*
   Bare hands leave fingerprints! Wear gloves.
4. *Thou shalt become a garbage collector!*
   Once your victim places his trash outside his home/office for pickup, it is legal for you to pick it up yourself. You can learn a lot about your mark by sifting through his papers and such. The pros do it all the time.

10

5. *Thou shalt bide thy time before activating a revenge plot!*
Give the victim time to forget about you and what he's done to wrong you. Getting even too soon makes it easier for him to discover who's doing it!

6. *Thou shalt secure a "mail drop" address in another another city!*
You don't want revenge mail being traced back to your residence/home, do you?

7. *Thou shalt learn everything there is to know about thy victim!*
The best revenge schemes/plans are hatched by people who know their victims better than their victims know themselves.

8. *Thou shalt pay cash all the time in a revenge plot!*
Checks, money orders, etc., can be traced back to you. Cash cannot!

9. *Thou shalt trade with merchants who have never heard of you!*
Do business with people only once when involved in a revenge plot. You can wear a disguise so the people you are involved with will have trouble identifying you in a legal confrontation.

10. *Thou shalt never threaten thy intended victim!*
Why warn your intended victim that you are going to get even? When bad things begin to happen to your victim, whether or not you caused them, your victim will remember your threat, and he or she will set out to even the score with *you*.

11. *Thou shalt not leave evidence lying around, however circumstantial!*
If you are thought to be actively engaged in having fun at your mark's expense, the authorities may visit you. Thus, it would be prudent not to have any books by Hayduke or Chunder at home or in the office.

HOW TO USE THIS WONDERFUL BOOK

I have arranged these subjects both by method and mark, listing them alphabetically. In addition to using the obvious subject headings, you can also do a cross-reference of your own. Or you can adapt a method listed for one mark for another mark or situation. Thus, these subjects become as versatile as your own imagination.

While this mix 'n match versatility is a standard item here, the personalized nasty touch is still the best. Another effective part of this business is the anticipation of further damage after your initial attack. This is grand psychological warfare.

CAUTION

The schemes, tricks, scams, stunts, cons, and scenarios presented here are for information and amusement purposes only. It is not my intent that you use this book as a manual or trickster's cookbook. I certainly don't expect that anyone who reads this book would actually ever *do* any of the things described here.

This book is written to entertain and inform readers, not to instruct or persuade them to commit any illegal act. Given my own mild disposition, I could hardly tell someone else to make any of these tactics operational.

Consider the case of mistaken vengeance that took place in Vienna, Austria, in 1985, when Leopold Renner thought his wife was cheating on him because he saw her holding hands with another man. The shocked husband stuffed twenty-seven of her live, exotic pets—one after another—into the churning garbage disposal. Down went screaming parakeets, hamsters, mice, and tarsiers into a gushy gruel feeding into the sewage drains.

Fact: His wife Frieda was holding the hand of her brother, whom she had not seen in a dozen years, and was bringing him home to meet her husband. True story.

Please read this book with that reference in mind. And remember; many lawyers are a great deal like rats and weasels, sniffing and crawling around, looking for sneaky passageways and tunnels through the soil of civilization's laws. But, as with rats and weasels, we humans can sometimes make use of these lawyers.

ACID

Relax flower parents (née flower children of the Sixties), I'm not doing blotter acid here. It's nitric acid that's on our agenda and, thanks to The Razor, also on your mark's clothing.

The usual low-intensity revengefare is not The Razor's style. He doesn't go for low-risk, low-cost stunts like dye and bleach; he wants to eat whole holes in the mark's ego-covering. Hence, nitric acid.

"You get eight to twelve ounces of it from a chemical supply house," The Razor relates. "Test it first on some old rags so you can get an idea of dose and fire rates. Use an eyedropper for your delivery system.

"After you've saturated a spot or two on your test rags, let them sit for an hour or so. Check them. This will give you a true appreciation for just how valuable a weapon nitric acid is to your efforts.

"In the field on an actual search-and-destroy mission, you'll know just how much acid to squirt surreptitiously on your mark's clothing. It will eat away all of the fabric."

The Razor says you can use larger doses of nitric acid on heater or air conditioning vents, which will really stink out your mark's home or office. He also told me how he dosed the office snoop 'n gossip who had several paybacks coming from a lot of people.

"I dampened the seat of her office chair with the acid a few moments before she was due in. She flopped her fat ass down on that chair and never noticed the dampness. A short while later the lady got up to move to another office and her skirt just sort of fell apart, as did the back of her underwear. She screamed and ran into the bathroom."

Eventually she was able to get a co-worker to fetch replacement clothing. The Razor reports that this woman has been much more civil to co-workers since "the incident."

Grizzled suggests that you can sometimes play Switcheroo with acids. For example, he says, "It is so pleasant and convenient that carmakers place the battery and the radiator so close together. That way it's very easy for you to play Switcheroo with your mark's car fluids."

What Grizzled suggests is to put battery acid in the radiator and undiluted antifreeze solution in the battery.

AGE

Jimmy Carter discovered age as a weapon of revenge. He worked with a truly nasty woman whom Jimmy called a mean bitch. I guess that means she is a female of a dog, or, perhaps, vice versa. Anyway, Jimmy dreamed of getting back at this genderized bully. Then he found out that she was very sensitive about her age and that she was passing into the big 30 that week.

Jimmy thought an office celebration would be in order, especially if he could make it seem as if someone else, a minor secondary mark, would get the eventual blame for the stunt. He did it all, with tacky being the marching order for the day.

"Naturally, I paid cash for everything but set up all the plans and reservations in the secondary mark's name," Jimmy told me. "I had Mr. Balloon deliver thirty of their most gaudy-awful Mylar balloons right to the office. He was followed by Mr. Party with a gross-looking cake with thirty candles. Telegrams followed, bogus, of course, from the mayor, the governor, and the President."

Jimmy added that variations could have included inflated and personalized condoms instead of balloons, or hiring several all-the-way strippers. As an after-action report, Jimmy notes that the lady in his office had a change of attitude after the birthday party.

AIRLINES

As this book is being written, it's hard to pick who is less popular: Iran, Hitler, or the U.S. airlines. For the moment, let's share this little plan to make the skies seem a bit more friendly. At least at first glance.

Everyone knows how the nice airlines have copies of current periodicals available for passengers. Current copies of *Time, Newsweek, U.S. News & World Report*, and others are placed inside stiff-bound plastic or board covers and made available to passengers.

Here comes the hook. You want to get back at an airline for something they did or didn't do to or for you. Before boarding the plane, stop at an adult book shop and buy three or four truly sleazy, gross magazines...stuff with titles like *Pederast's Delight In The Playground* or *Tammy Does Farm Animals*...you get the picture.

Sneak these smutty mags onto the aircraft in your carry-on and then replace the as-issued magazines with them. Sit back and watch some horrified passenger discover what has happened. Maybe you could also stick a label on the cover that says "This wonderful magazine donated courtesy of ...." and name your least favorite politician, actor, televangelist, or whoever.

Here's another trick. If you call and sound hysterical enough, you can claim an ongoing personal emergency to cancel airline reservations for your mark. My Honduran friend Papel Higienico adds that you can also accomplish the same thing by calling and claiming to be a police officer, an

EMT person, doctor, etc. The secret here is to sound authoritative—use jargon, ID yourself by a number as well as name, etc. You can also use a set-up number for them to call back to verify the claim...easily enough done.

Papel has also used the telephone to switch airlines and/or flights for his mark. He carries a small, hand-held set to the airport and plugs it into an empty jack at a check-in counter.

"I wear a fake ID badge and stand there with my clipboard," Papel relates. "I call another airline or even the one I am using and switch the mark's reservations all around. I travel enough that I know the procedures, the jargons, and the codes. It's easy and the mark will always blame the airline."

ANSWERING MACHINES

I don't know why people dislike these useful devices so much. Maybe it's some kind of personal insecurity. You can have fun with them, as good friend Russell Straley points out. The best part about Russell's plan is that you can customize your stunt for almost any situation or caller. Furthermore, his plan is on the other side of the telephone, the callee getting back at the caller.

Russell explains, "You simply pretend to be your own answering machine. You answer the phone in a mechanical way, maybe with a little electronic hum in the background — a turned-down radio will do that.

"Sometimes people leave messages, sometimes not. You can respond however you wish to the message. Think about that! Blow people's minds, images, tempers. Refuse to become human. Be a thinking answering machine. I've done it. It freaks people."

ATOMIC LIGHTBULB

The Magic Z says this is the stunt you pull only on your worst enemy. He says it is devastating. The idea is to booby-trap your mark's electric light—office, bedroom, kitchen, bathroom, whatever. Here are Magic's steps.

1. Choose the bulb to work with (a 100-watter is best).

2. Using a propane torch at its very lowest level, gently soften the glass at the top of the bulb. Be gentle and careful; you don't want the bulb to break, just to soften.

3. When the bulb is softened, poke your finger to push in the top. Your goal is to make a 3/4-inch dent in the light bulb. Pour about five or six drops of gasoline into this dent.

4. Melt some candle wax in another container, then let it cool slightly. While it still pours, spread it over the gasoline-filled dent in the bulb. Be very sure the wax seals the dent totally. Let the whole thing harden ten hours.

5. Replace that bulb in your mark's light fixture.

When the mark turns that light on, it will take about five or ten minutes to activate. The filament will grow hot enough to ignite the gasoline, which is held in by the wax. The explosion will blow the hell out of everything connected with that system.

The Magic Z warns, "Use extreme caution."

And note the disclaimer on the copyright page of this book.

AUTOMOBILES

One of Stu's more juvenile pals decided it would be funny to try frying an egg on the roof of Stu's ride while our hero had his vehicle parked at work for the day. It was in the low nineties outside and the semi-cooked egg made a nasty mess on the car's finish.

"My response was simple, direct, and appropriate," Stu says. "I found this jerk's own car and had a nice helping of revenge. I took a raw egg, broke the shell gently, and let the insides slide equally gently into his car's gas tank."

Stu reveals that eventually the egg will get sucked into the fuel line and stop the engine. When the engine and pump shut down, the egg will probably float back out, ready for a repeat performance. Stu adds that this is a very difficult problem for the mark to discover.

Another culinary contribution to home auto care is this devious idea from Capt. Video, who has teamed with Aunt Jemima (or the maker of any instant pancake mix) to help you take revenge against your mark's motor vehicle. Always fastidious, Capt. Video says to be certain you prepare the pancake mixture properly, according to the instructions on the box.

"Then you pour that mixture on the engine block of your mark's vehicle, preferably while the block is hot. Have you any idea at all what that will stink like? You don't want to know," advises our video visionary.

That's neat—your mark can cook pancakes as he drives to work, school, or wherever.

Jim Simmons found that it was very easy to redirect the windshield-cleaner-fluid nozzle away from the intended direction and, instead, aim it toward the sidewalk, thus hitting pedestrians.

"I had a good pump, a stronger than normal pump on there, and was able to hit people fifteen to twenty feet away easily. I used that a lot when I was riding through places in town where people yelled at me or kids threw things or gave me the finger. It was neat."

Rather than spray marks, Grizzled found another use for the windshield system of his mark's car. He modifies the wipers slightly. His modification is to coat the wiper blade with one of the miracle-type super glues and some sand. He said that the rubber cement used to patch tires and some sandpaper grit will work fine, also.

Revengeful Chris has discovered the fun of locking gas caps. She says it works best when you know your mark is planning on driving for a long vacation or business trip. The inconvenience and delay for someone who's done her a real wrong are wonderful to think about.

"I really dig throwing away those keys and thinking about all the fury and frustration my mark is suffering," Chris says.

That is not unlike the work of Samurai Cat and Grid Warrior, who have found several things you can do to your mark's vehicle. One is to replace the radiator fluid with motor oil, which will cause a smelly mess. Then again, I recall my pal Dick Smegma telling me about substituting gasoline for radiator fluid...but, I digress. Samurai Cat and Grid Warrior have another scheme, this time for rear-wheel drive cars. It's a simple modification to the standard equipment power train.

The Cat says, "Remove three of the four bolts on the connection between the drive shaft and the rear axle. When the vehicle builds any torque, *boom*, the bolt will snap causing nasty things to happen to the vehicle."

For those of you with visions of your mark's car careening off the road, please reread the disclaimer in the beginning of the book.

By golly, it's Ray Heffer back again, this time with some snappy quickies for your mark's automobile. Here's Ray...

• Dump a handful of shredded cheese into the gas tank of the mark's car. Guess what happens next?

• Want to slash tires without attracting attention? Do the Heffer version of Rosa Klebb. Wrap several heavy-duty rubber bands around the toe end of your shoe. Insert a very sharp knife blade under the sole side. You can use electrical tape to secure the blade even more. Walk up to the tire and kick hell, and the air, out of it.

• Brown sugar gums up an engine far worse than refined white sugar.

If you need to get into a locked car or truck and don't have the necessary tools, The Blackmail Kid has a suggestion. He says, "On a lot of vehicles from 1986 back, door locks are easy. Locate the area about two or three inches directly under the door lock. Give this area a really solid and very good punch.

"I'm talking solid shot. You need to almost dent the metal. At the same time you'll open the door lock."

BALLOONS

Children are usually such innocent by-products. A balloon has always been a favorite play toy for a child, even for those of us who are growing down. Thus, the following stunt is dedicated to its early practitioners: Chris, Uncle David, The Good Colonel, Lyle & Tector, Brother George, Uncle Gerry, and Rusty.

The stunt is wonderfully guaranteed to upset parents, employers, employees, teachers, officers, and other humorless grown-ups. Here's how it works.

Take a child's small balloon of that sort we knew as "penny balloons." Stretch it loose so it will inflate easily. Clear one nostril vigorously, at least for beginners.

Now stuff the open end of the balloon into that nostril, shut your other nostril very tightly with your finger, then blow your nose hard. If you've done it properly, the balloon will inflate quite easily.

Your imagination will let you modify and grossify this stunt so as to tailor its impact for a specific audience; i.e., you might not wish to clean your inflation nostril before blowing up the balloon, thus adding solid materials to its interior.

A scholar as well as a tactical instructor, I was determined to learn the genesis of this stunt. As nearly as I could tell from research, it was first done by a seven-year-old boy as a Stupid Human Trick on "The David Letterman Show."

BANKS

With some wrong done to him lying on his mind, Rusty McBenge found a delightful way to deposit some grief with interest upon his mark. Of course, you have to practice some sleight of hand before you slight the mark's no-account mind. Let's let Rusty tell the how of things.

"If your mark has an account in a bank that issues preprinted personal deposit slips, obtain a supply of them. I'll leave the how of that detail up to your imagination...it's not all that tough.

"These slips are imprinted with that magnetic-coded numbering system that automatically credits the mark's account with each deposit filed. Your next step is easy. Just scatter a few of these slips in with the regular deposit slips in the bank lobby before peak business periods. Or you can have some friends fill in a few and deposit them.

"It will not take bank authorities long to find out that something has gone drastically wrong as soon as the first few complaints come in from irate customers whose deposits never showed up in their own accounts. The bank computer will quickly locate the mark's account."

At this point, I suspect, Rusty's mark will start to feel that world of federal-interest-in-him dung closing over his head. It also might teach that mark a valuable lesson about fiscal fitness.

BEER

Beer belongs, abuse it. There are so many nice things I could say about beer as my favorite drink of immoderation, often chased by shots of tequila. That's the way it was one night down on the Maricón River, somewhere near the village of Culo Salchichón. LTC Mac, Col. Mills, Lester Scrotum, old Mr. Graham, and I had gotten there from Nogales the day before and were busy murdering our brain cells with myriad flagons of drinkypoo when Scrotum brought up the Great Corona Coup of 1987.

Corona is this great Mexican beer. Indeed, almost all Mexican beers are far Superior (yes, a pun) to American brands because they are real and not manufactured for some half-assed bland national taste. Anyway, someone, a business competitor or some teetotaling American (there are few Latino nondrinkers—most of them nuns), spread a very effective rumor that Corona was a pissy-flavored beer, literally.

Not true. I know because I donated a lot of time and a lot of my liver to checking out the rumor that year. As it comes from the brewery in Mexico City, Corona is great, grand beer.

There are, however, some lessons to be learned here: one, rumors are usefully harmful, as Corona learned when their sales dropped off a whole lot before a public relations/ advertising blitz cured their reputation; two, you can probably start rumors, also; three, maybe you know someone whose beer does need to be used as a urinal in payment for something done to you.

That serves well enough as an introduction to Madman Mike, a friend who spends time visiting our foreign neighbors as part of his career. Mike says that as hosts and friendlies, the French rank right alongside herpes. Unlike AIDS, nobody ever died from herpes, but who'd want to go back? The same may be said of France, according to Mike, a cosmopolitan sort who is multilingual.

"My fiancée had asked a French restaurant owner if several ladies who were on their way with us to visit Lourdes could use his bathroom, which was locked. He practically spat at her and said 'NO, you have not bought enough here. It is only for good French customers, not stupid American tourists.'"

Mike adds that his fiancée had been speaking to the man in English but he responded in French with his blast about Americans. Mike spat back in French and said that he would handle the matter his own way. His group left and continued their trip to Lourdes.

"On the way back we stopped and I went in that same place. The man didn't recognize me and I simply grunted and pointed at a beer. He served it and wandered away. It was dark in there that evening and as customers wandered away I quickly grabbed their glasses off the bar and surreptitiously urinated in each glass and replaced it on the bar. I left."

BIKERS

I hang out with some grand bikers. I also try to avoid the ones who strut around all cocky, like an armed guard in a prison camp for blind quadriplegics. So does The Devil's Advocate, who writes with some suggestions for these preening parasites.

- Start the rumor that your biker-mark is a machine thief. This will poison his reputation very quickly.
- Help the rumor along by either getting some stolen parts or steal some yourself to plant on his property, home, whatever.
- Write letters in the biker-mark's name to *Supercycle* and/or *Easyriders* and denounce the bike life or bike ladies, or stick up for helmet laws, gays, etc.

Easily, though, our hats and helmets are off to The Hat for a stunt he orchestrated some years ago to help out a crippled pal who was being terrorized by a strong-arm druggie. It started with the druggie dealing from the cripple's place of business. Being they were both bikers, the cripple pleaded with the big/bad guy to stop dealing and to leave. The muscle responded by punching the smaller, crippled man and sexually going after his wife.

The law was called and the bad guy got forty-five days. Everyone figured it was all over. Two days after his release, however, the bad guy shows up and empties a pistol into the crippled brother's shop, nearly striking people inside.

"Some of the others wanted to waste him, but I had another idea," recalled The Hat. "So we set him up. Got the wife of one of our brothers to set him up in a bar. We drugged him with Seconal, then we got nasty."

They stripped the mark and placed him in a large, wooden packing crate, securing his arms, hands, and legs with surgical tape. They then put a plastic hose into his mouth, using tape to hold it in place. The other end was put into a gallon plastic jug of water which they'd spiked with LSD and amphetamines.

"One of our guys was a ringer for this jerk, so we had him dress in the mark's clothes and made sure he was seen around some of the other bars that day. Then we all took the crate to a motor freight place and had the mark look-alike send it, containing the still-sleeping real mark, away," The Hat said.

"The crate was marked 'PERISHABLE...DO NOT FREEZE' and 'OPEN IMMEDIATELY.' The contents were listed as 'SHELLED NUTS.' We were told it would take three days to arrive."

And where did they send this parcel? Why, to the State Hospital for the Criminally Insane.

The Hat says nobody ever heard of or from the mark ever again and they have no idea what became of him. He is also not aware of any legal problems, statute of limitations, or anything else, so he is being very vague about locales. I understand.

Isn't that a wonderfully warm story of justice overcoming evil? Notice that nobody needed lawyers, bullycoppers, or anything else to make it work? Ain't true democracy grand?

BLACK OLIVES

According to Dick Smegma, head of the Hayduke Institute's R&D lab, black olives do not disintegrate, digest, or change their original shape when they are ingested whole. If you swallow them whole without mushing them, black olives will come out your pukki in the same shape as they went in your mouth.

I'm certain you already know what Mr. Smegma and I are thinking. However, being a practical scientist, he has some workable uses all ready for consumer disclosure. For example, your recycled olives could be used at an unfavorite salad bar, a mark's home salad bar, a gift pizza to someone, or even placed in random fashion in a resealable jar and given to someone.

Mr. Smegma also suggests you could experiment with other foods to learn more about this interesting natural phenomenon. Corn is one that I know about. Isn't this fun, boys and girls?

BOMB

Isn't that a wonderful word? It's so descriptive and so fun-laden in all its glory and meaning. Actually, this suggestion, coming from chemists Rob M. and Bryan S., has the full formal name of The Hindenburg Bomb, and here's how it works.

Fill a Coke bottle three-quarters full of Liquid Plumber and add a small piece of aluminum foil to it. Put a balloon over the neck of the bottle and let the resultant gas rise into the balloon.

Insert a *long* length of cannon fuse under the end of the balloon, being careful not to let much hydrogen escape. Then light the length of fuse.

At this point, the guys say to *run like hell 'til you drop* because these babies really explode. Hence their full, formal name. We can think of lots of ways to use The Hindenburg Bomb other than just for personal explosion amusement.

Perhaps less violent, but then, perhaps not (ahhh, such is the nature of that lovely word *bomb*), is the handiwork of Capt. Video. Actually, I've known about this one for years, having had family close to the Kentucky, West Virginia, and Pennsylvania mining scenes in the thirties and forties. But, speaking of eyesores, I have digressed.

The Captain says to add about a quarter pound of carbide to a large plastic bag. Add a long fuse. Then add a half gallon of water before you seal the bag very thoroughly and quickly. If you have sealed the mixture properly, a great deal of explosive gas will be created. The resultant explosion is

31

not only very loud, it can be quite destructive.

Back in the old days, folks close to the mines used to go fishing with this type of rig. It was much quicker than lines and bait, being more adaptable to feeding families than sport ego. It was a forerunner to the military custom of grenade fishing. Now, that reminds me of the time...

Meanwhile, back in the present, Capt. Video suggests "Bull's-eye Smokeless Pistol Powder" as a wonderful product for people interested in demolitions or other pyrotechnic games. I concur with the Captain, but be aware that this is also nasty stuff if handled improperly. Used properly, however, it makes a splendid filler to load up Ping-Pong balls, paper tubes, toilet paper cores, or whatever.

This stuff is pretty vigorous when it goes off, so stay away from it and *don't* use it to turn your mark's charcoal grill or trash incinerator into a backyard bomb. Also, watch how you store it and read the label cautions carefully. It is available in many gun shops.

BOOKS

Kaysing, Bill. *Privacy*. Fountain Valley, CA: Eden Press, 1986.

This fine tome explains the entire topic well, including how to protect your privacy and how to invade that of other people. It's a good book and is also available through Paladin Press.

Levine, Michael. *The New Address Book*. New York: Putnam Publishing Group, 1988.

A must reference for Haydukers, this book contains contact addresses for celebrities, political figures, corporate execs, and public company execs. It has phone numbers too. It's wonderful.

Rapp, Burt. *Shadowing & Surveillance*. Port Townsend, WA: Loompanics Press, 1986.

All good Haydukers need to know these techniques, as well as how to use them to avoid being the subject of someone else's research.

_____. *Undercover Work.* Port Townsend, WA: Loom-
    panics Press, 1986.

There are a lot of manuals in this field and I like this one a
good bit. Also, the subject is very useful in my line of
activity.

BOSSES

My friend Terri Lee used to work for a really mean bear of a boss who was a real grouch and a bastard for docking people if they were a few moments late for work. Terri and her pal Cissy plotted and planned for ways of correcting the boss's nasty preoccupation with time.

"One of the things we did was to drop toothpicks, paper clips, and folded Scotch tape down into the card slot when nobody was looking," Terri told me.

She said it messed up the machine and forced the boss to come around and ask people when they came in so he could write in the time-check information by hand while the time clock was being repaired.

"When it was back in service we waited two days, then dropped a condom wrapper in the slot. This time the boss called a meeting and asked who had the problem with the time clock. Finally, he admitted he'd been overdoing it and promised he'd cool it if we'd stop messing with the clock. That was that."

Terri had another boss during one of her other lives, a true racist redneck. She told me, "The man hated black people for no reason, sense, brains, or passion. He was color-stricken, brainblind. He was also a pig who hit on women and used his power to unfair, slimeball advantage.

"The guy had no class and no real power. That insecurity is why he was such a prick to all the little people who worked for him. I mean, this is a guy with his name on his office door, but he didn't flush the company toilet without checking upstairs," Terri told me, as she explained how she nailed him.

"He had to drive through a predominantly black section of the city to get to work and I knew I could use that. I went to a custom printer of bumper stickers and got three done that said HONK FOR HONKIE POWER, I ♥ KKK, and BURN BLACKS. I put all three on his car. Some real fun started, including a brick through the back window, paint on the side, and eggs all over it. He was livid and called the police."

Terri said that when the detective team came to investigate, one was a black officer. He saw the bumper stickers and pointed them out to the boss, who was furiously flabbergasted. The investigators seemed to be amused. Terri was amused.

So am I.

BRATS

Childhood is too much fun to be wasted on children. Nonetheless, they are upon us, sometimes like the locusts which used to plague our much earlier ancestors. Bryan Fear used to babysit for family and neighbors. Sometimes he was stuck with awful brats who figured because he was family or a neighbor friend, he could be bullied and otherwise abused. These kids didn't count on Bryan's brutal mind.

"One nasty kid burned two of my expensive textbooks simply by tossing them into the fireplace. Some kids are neat and nice. I seemed to get the other kind," Bryan said.

One of these kids, a perfect argument for retroactive abortion rights, finally goaded Bryan to action.

"I finally convinced the little asshole to go to bed. While he was in the bathroom I brought a pan of cold water filled with ice cubes into his bedroom. The pan and I hid under his bed. I submerged my hand in the pan, holding it there until he arrived and began to crawl into his bed.

"I reached up and snatched tight on his ankle and began to pull him off the bed and toward me, all the while moaning. My hand was so cold that I could barely feel it. I know that he did, though.

"The kid let out a pants-wetting scream and tore away from my grip. He ran from the room, screaming for me. I let him rip all over the house, terrified, screaming for help. I calmly returned the pan to the kitchen and sat quietly in the den as I heard him running all over the house, top to bottom, screaming for me. He finally came into the den, crying and

37

shaking."

The kid demanded that Bryan check for monsters under the bed. Of course, there were none. At this point, Bryan used blackmail psychology to insure that the kid would behave. Otherwise, he wouldn't check for monsters and monsters might return. Bryan told the parents about the child's nightmare.

I would imagine this would work well with multiple children, too. You can always spread the terror evenly and while one is running around seeking help, you can grab others.

Happily, Bryan Fear lives up to his name.

BUREAUCRATS

If you're looking here for instant revenge, what you're going to get instead is a caution. Be very careful of irritating the little cogs in a bureaucracy, especially if these people are in charge of records, computers, or other weapons that can be turned on you. Think about it! Also, it is often systems and the bosses who dictate them that cause your problems; it's not always the little person with whom you might deal personally.

As Madman Mike, a military vet, points out, "Be careful when you abuse a clerk. Sometimes, what I call 'The Deadly Triangle' gets after you."

Most vets of any bureaucracy—corporate, educational, military, governmental, etc.—will recognize The Deadly Triangle. It is an alliance of three clerical friends in three different departments of the bureaucracy. They conspire to punish you for abusing one of the trio by involving you in the flytrap of all three departments.

Mike says, "Let's say you cross a billeting clerk. Your shot record might get lost in medical and you might come up short at payroll...all due to 'computer error,' of course."

On the positive side, if you know a way into the web of The Deadly Triangle at your mark's nearest bureaucracy, perhaps a loudly voiced complaint, report, or nasty comment on your mark's behalf and in his or her name would be helpful. But be careful. While many bureaucrats are losers with the unctuous whine of overused bacon fat on low heat, they can still be dangerous, as can a cornered rat or jackal.

CABBAGE PATCH MANNEQUINS

Building these custom friends can be creatively ugly, but enjoyable. According to Carla Savage, the brains behind this idea, their use can be even more so. First, Carla says you have to personally try this to appreciate how realistic the effect is.

"It's really easy, too," Carla explains. "You just stuff nylon stockings with cotton. Use two pairs for arms and legs, then add more for whatever body parts you wish."

Carla adds that you don't have to be an artist to create the human contours and features desired for that perfect effect. You are limited only by your own imagination and the number of stockings and amount of cotton you have. Carla says not to forget clothes, paints, Magic Marker, and other human like disguise.

What can you do with these life-sized, if not lifelike, new friends? Here are some thoughts from Carla:

• Impressing the neighbors...how will your new friends look on creative display on the mark's lawn? Do the words "Kama Sutra" come to mind?

• Is it Christmas? Wouldn't it be fun to add some new players to your community-mark's Nativity Scene?

• Do you remember those posters and calendars with the zodiac sexual positions? This would be an interesting variation on The Twelve Days of Christmas.

• Or perhaps you could use your cotton-stocking friends

to adorn park statues. Some creative sexual positioning ideas jump to mind right away.

• You could also produce an anatomically erect penis using the same basic products. Could this be shipped or delivered to a mark or markess with devastating effect?

Good friend Carla has field-tested this idea in several configurations and loves it. She gives this her personal Good Hayduking Seal of Approval. I trust this wonderful lady's judgment about everything. Need we add more?

CABLE TV

Hilda Rexer had a neighbor whose cable TV reception ruined her on-air reception due to some oddball electronics nonsense. Rather than work out some friendly sort of neighborly arrangement or compromise, Hilda's neighbor ignored the protest and situation. Hilda used the telephone and the local cable company to get even.

"I called the cable company and used my neighbor's name to cancel her pay-channel selections. I substituted an adult channel for one of the canceled ones, explaining I was doing it as a gift for my husband," Hilda told me.

The matter was finally straightened out. Hilda said it took five weeks, including some grim calls from the nasty neighbor, before the lady agreed to be nice. Hilda waited four more weeks of nice, then zapped the other lady's cable outlet with an electromagnet just for fun.

CAMPERS

In a team, herd, or species concept, campers often consider themselves a family of sorts. Sometimes other campers take advantage of the generosity that goes without asking among true campers. Sick Sid the Avenger recalled how his group paid back one of these take-advantage groups.

"These bozos borrowed everything with little repayment. It was almost as if they came camping and deliberately left their gear and supplies at home," Sid recalls. "This one group kept on borrowing stuff until they just began to take without even asking. That did it."

The remedy was simple. As the other campers kept borrowing the bug juice for the nightly invasion of biting crawlies and fliers, Sid replaced the bug repellent solution with a mixture of lemon juice and sugar water.

"Ahhh," Sid recalls, "even now, in my mind I can hear the shouts of frustration, horror, and finally anguish as those little insects helped us to even a debt."

CARPETS

I'll bet it grinds your gut when some careless slob drops a cigarette or spills a drink, chili sauce, or the contents of his stomach on your rug. Dick Smegma discovered a nice way of returning the favor to your messy mark. Dick says if you slowly and carefully pour liquid bleach, with chlorine, on a carpet, it will permanently stain it a lighter color or totally wash out the color.

Dick thinks it amusing to gain access to your mark's carpeting when he isn't there and pour the undiluted bleach directly onto the carpet so that the discoloration spells obscene, racial, or ethnic words and phrases. Actually, you could get creative about this, bringing the mark's family into the messages you're writing on the rug.

CB RADIO

It's common knowledge that the state police, highway patrols, and other law enforcement officials monitor CB channels 9 and 19 on a regular basis. Usually, the result is help or aid in an emergency or other frightening situation.

However, it isn't abusing that help if you were to create a fictitious conversation with another good buddy out there. Of course, if you are a good actor/actress, Mr. Poleeece doesn't need to know it's just you doing only one side of an imaginary talk on the old CB.

Relate hilarious stories about your mark breaking speed laws, drinking and driving, littering, showing Mr. Johnson to a group of little school girls, peeing on the parish steps, and so on. I'm sure you can do something to get the attention of the officers.

In fact, my old pal Catzo Cignetti did just that when he got on his highly mobile CB and started bad-mouthing the local gendarmes in the name of his mark. He pretended to be drunk and got really abusive and personal. He started to name some troopers and relate in some detail what he was doing to their wives and house pets while they were on duty.

"I knew this jerk of a mark, who'd been making my wife's life miserable at her job, always got drunk during Happy Hour at a local bar. So, just before Happy Hour ended, I did this CB attack on the police in his name. I ended up by challenging them to come down to the bar and stand up to me as men and I'd whip their asses one by one," Catzo told me.

We can all imagine what happened when Mr. Mark stumbled out of that bar that evening, can't we?

If you don't want to go to all of that fun, you can simply report your mark for speeding, drunk driving, racing, etc. You just get on the CB channel that your local road police monitor and report your mark for breaking the law. Mention his car type and color and maybe a partial on the license. Of course it will be investigated. It was a state police officer who suggested this scam to me in the first place.

As noted elsewhere in this tome (see Farts), CB radios are a grand medium for sharing your bodily function noises with the general public. According to that grand old columnist from San Francisco, Herb Caen, other body parts interest CBers on the California freeways. Herb writes, "We should tell people who hang those stupid yellow, diamond-shaped signs in their cars that, according to an overheard CB conversation, 'Them damn baby-on-board signs make great aim-at targets for freeway shooters.'"

That ought to worry a lot of people. Or, as my old pal from our Mexico days, Jack Beasley, would say, "That'll make your butt tighter than a bull's at the height of biting fly season." You got that right, Jack.

CENSORS

Lust, or poor people's polo, has always held a fascination for me. That's also true of my good friend Paul Wiltbuns, a former minister who found sexual overdrive so much fun that he gave up crusading against it and began to enjoy himself. Paul found a grand way to defeat those evil-minded censors who always want to put their "no's" into our pleasure.

"I modified an old stunt of yours, George," Paul told me over a couple of lemonades recently. "I ordered the sleaziest porn I could find. I ordered it COD in the name of each of the local censors who'd been loudly trying to rape the First Amendment in our town.

"But the kicker is that I used the very same address for each censor...the home address of the preacher who ran their operation from his fundamentalist church, the First Rectalfied Church of Reagan/Meese."

Paul says the local postal officials were both amused and annoyed. He says the preacher got livid on his weekly radio show on the local Bible-banger station, WIMP. The town newspaper carried a story about the incidents. Paul waited two months for the brimstone and smoke to clear, then did it all over again.

Meanwhile, in Canada, many readers tell me that some customs and postal authorities have banned my books, considering them to be "dangerous to the well-being of Canadian citizens." I couldn't believe it. I called their version of the Mind Police and found that it was true. Wow.

Dr. Deviant found a way to get back at the Canadian censors. He got various book catalogs which contained books either officially banned or which probably soon would be banned from that bastion of northern North American press freedom.

"Using friends and cutouts, I safely ordered a bunch of the banned books in this dude's name and for his home address. I ordered them COD and included a faked letter on phony 'official' letterhead stating that 'I' was a government official who wanted to review these books.

"About a week before they were due to arrive, I called law enforcement officials, including customs, postal, and police, to report, as a good citizen whose name will not be used, that Czar Bookburner was trying to use his official station to obtain evil literature."

As with my friend Paul's stunt, Dr. Deviant's scam made the newspapers in his town. According to the press stories, the closed-minded official had a lot of explaining to do. I should hope so. Personally, I'd burn these evil censors at the stake if I were in charge. Sadly, I'm not...not yet, anyway.

CHEMICALS

Many loyal funfolk have written for a source of the great stench producer, butyl mercaptan. Thanks to my famed New Englander pal Squeamish we now have a source for this comedy chemical. Order it from The Hatpin, P.O. Box 6144, Santa Fe, NM 87502. You're welcome.

Another friend, Jimmy Carter, being the good chemical expert that he is, passes along a warning to Haydukers who are unsophisticated with chemistry. He notes that ammonia and chlorine bleach are two useful and safe revenge products, *if kept separate*. Jimmy says *do not combine the two!*

If you mix these two products together, they will form a deadly gas which is very similar to one used by some elements within our own government to kill people. *Be warned!!*

CHILD ABUSE

If I were a true cynic, I would define child abuse as coming back to live with your parents after you've already left the nest once. Then there is the other kind, the nasty kind. Most states have very strong laws to punish these monsters who beat or sexually molest little kids. Many states have child protection laws which mandate that teachers, nurses, doctors, and other professionals report suspected child abuse situations to the law. A version of the good Samaritan concept protects the anonymity and liability of the informant.

Now, suppose you have a mark who is one of those folks mandated to report child abuse. Why not have that mark report a case that is an obvious fraud or that is so suspect as to make it ridiculous, like, for example, fingering his ex-spouse or a person incapable of such acts. The idea is to make the mark look like a vengeful sort of jerk in the eyes of the law. And, as any officer will tell you, they remember things like that even if they can't do anything about it legally or at the time. That means your mark will have a mark against him or her.

CIA

When it comes to spying on good loyal Americans, the CIA's into it right up to the tip of its paranoid little dagger. But when it comes to sharing information with We The People, the Agency folks do not squander the English language. They dole out useful information about as often as Charlie Manson has kinky sex with a Barbie Doll. But they can be useful, according to Houdini.

He had an especially annoying associate who also had a very suspicious mind. Houdini decided to drive him across suspicious and into paranoia. Here is what Houdini did.

"With a very fine rubber stamp utilizing the CIA seal and the Langley address, I carefully stamped it on the return portion of the front of an ordinary postal card. On the back of the card, using an IBM typewriter from a public library near where I go to school, I typed a terse message, addressed it, and mailed it to my mark."

Houdini's message was:

You have exactly ten days to correct any alleged inaccuracy in the criminal conduct file report on yourself that we sent you pursuant to espionage laws Title 18, USC Secs 793 and 794. Final notice.

The card was signed simply by a typed line: Legal Staff. Houdini warns you to be careful of fingerprints. He says the mark's father consulted an attorney to investigate. Of course, the CIA never admits anything, bewildered or not. I

51

bet Houdini's mark *does* have a file opened by the CIA after this stunt.

CLEANING SUPPLIES

There are times when the janitorial and cleaning supplies of a mark are not only susceptible to revenge, they beg for it. Back when he was a student, Sick Sid the Avenger found he got tired of doing free cleaning for the school because the authorities had sent him to detention hall for being a class clown.

"Hey, I didn't mind doing homework or reading, but I'll be damned if I was going to do manual labor for the school. I complained and even mentioned liability if I were hurt on the job. You know what the Principrick did? He gave me two more hours of detention," Sid says.

"When I got off detention I let things ride for a month. Then, one afternoon I got into the janitorial supply closet with a key I had boosted earlier. I switched the paper labels between cans of industrial aerosol cleaner with those of spray paint. I added bleach to some of the containers of Windex. I put light oil in others. I used Drano in others. Charcoal dust went into some of the furniture polish containers used in the Big Honcho's offices."

As an aside, let me add that you could also exchange labels between cans of aerosol static cling eliminator and those of spray-on dry lubricant. Your mark will never note the difference until the clothes are put back on.

Yucko-Neato.

COMPACT DISCS

Although The Sperminator did this payback with regular records, it will also work with CDs, especially if we're going to be technologically up to date. As usual, a major-mail order record club badly screwed up their financial files related to The Sperminator's account. Letters and calls did no good and he finally had to pay an attorney some money to get the club off his back. Then he really got interested in setting the record straight.

The Sperminator found one of those "ten CDs, records or tapes for a buck" ads from his former club. He filled it out and ordered some of the very popular current numbers likely to be stocked by most record stores.

"I wanted the money, man, so stick with me here," our hero snarled by way of explanation.

He used a vacant house in another neighborhood for his return address and his telephone number was that for a rural pay phone in another county. Naturally, he used a fake name, choosing one of his enemies as a secondary mark.

It took about three weeks for the ten records to arrive at the drop. The Sperminator picked them up and went to the most expensive record stores in town.

"I explained that I'd gotten these records as a birthday gift and that I wanted to return them because I didn't have a player, or that I already had them. They're sealed in plastic, obviously new, and perhaps you've managed to swindle a sales receipt."

He says his only snag so far has been that twice the store

54

wouldn't give back money without a receipt, which he couldn't get. He settled for new merchandise on an exchange basis.

COMPUTERS

A lot of people are slaves to computers, voluntarily or no, actively or no. And computers are a lot of work, too. Once some fool was messing with The Razor's computer life, which is like teasing Lady MacBeth after a hard day's knife (sorry if you don't like literary puns).

The Razor starts off easy with his revenge. He suggests a total rearrangement of cable hookups from the main terminal to the various peripheral devices, like the printer, disk drives, monitor, etc.

"It's just harassment, but so few folks ever really check the hookups," says The Razor. "So you rearrange things and the computer blows, won't work, or works oddly. Most marks will head for the repair service before looking at the hookups."

On a more serious level, The Razor suggests that you hit the mark where his computer lives—in its chips. He adds, "Chips are the elongated black objects that appear to be stuck to the green circuitry. Chips are easily removed for normal service work. You have other plans for them, however."

The idea is to remove the computer's cover and remove a few chips. Or place the wrong chips in the wrong holders. Or coat them with clear nail polish. Perhaps the best thing to do is to simply take them away and dispose of them. Replace the computer cover and let the mark wonder what happened. The usual result is a hefty repair charge. As Thorne Smith once wrote, "Life is just one long dirty trick."

There is also mien to Razor's mean. One of his high school teachers cast lustful attention upon Razor's lady friend. A most unhappy situation soon erupted, causing chaos in all directions. A heady sort, Razor headed for the teacher's computer system, the man's true love.

"I borrowed a couple of his private work diskettes and took 'em home. I removed the medium from one of them. That's the shiny black plastic stuff that stores data. I replaced the medium with some very fine black sandpaper. Some thin, fast-drying glue held the sandpaper in place in the diskette holder sandwich," Razor related.

He replaced the computer-killer floppy in the teacher's files. He also thought it might be fun to do the same thing if the man ever crossed the line of professional behavior again.

"He didn't have time for a while. He was too busy explaining why his diskette ruined school equipment. Not only was he trying to screw students, but he'd been using the school's computer equipment to do his own personal work. My custom disk erased that, and it booted him into a lot of hassle with his bosses."

Syd Fudd is a computer technician who was fired from a company because one of his co-workers made a costly mistake. She was not fired because she was a Token from the Minority Hiring Quota Bank and the company had many government contracts. Syd said she was also a very pretty 39D. Sexist, for sure, but true.

In any case, as a going away present, one of Syd's angry pals wrote an Accounts Receivable program with a built-in self-destruct "virus" into the company's records with the time-release formula set to go off in thirty days. It worked, and the result was seventeen days of costly chaos in which much confusion accrued and many dollars were lost.

A survivor, Syd is doing just fine, but he still doesn't consider it a fair trade. The company's opinion was not sought.

Doc Sarvis, a computer expert, relates that computers,

laser printers, and other desktop publishing materials make it very easy for you to create all sorts of bogus letterheads and other printed materials. You are limited only by your imagination and/or conscience.

"For example, you could have an official medical form or letterhead inform your mark's employer, family, school, unit, or whoever, that his or her most recent examination showed HTLV-3 positive, an indication of exposure to AIDS. Nasty, but effective," Doc explains.

At one point, a supposed friend stole computer programming from Bryan S. and Rob M. They waited for a while, then set up their mark for the big payback.

"Through a cutout we let him know he could get a free copy of the latest program disk. But before we arranged for him to get it, we modified it a bit," the guys related. "You pour some clear nail polish remover onto some clipped off match heads. Crush the mixture until you can't see the heads and everything is gooey."

The stunt is to then paint the substance on the disk you are giving the mark. They did it to their mark. The payback is that when the mark boots the loaded disk, it boots his computer drive really hard.

Enough nasty. It's time for silly fun. Thanks to the comical genius of Dale McKinnon, president of the Modern Advisory Institute, we now have access to some wonderful computer-generated *Pranks*. Mr. McKinnon's outfit sells software known as *Pranks*, which is a collection of relatively harmless practical joke programs. I've used *Pranks* and some of the selections are grandly hilarious. For example, there is one menu selection called "Printer Panic." Unknown and unplanned by the mark, it causes his or her printer to malfunction, spewing sheet after sheet of paper through the printer, like the machine was under the control of a poltergeist.

The idea behind *Pranks* is that you use McKinnon's

software to load your booby traps, gimmicks, insults, and surprises into your mark's PC. You program your "pranks" to function from the mark's normal prompt. You leave. The mark comes in, cranks up the old PC and hits the usual prompt. Thanks to *Pranks*, that's when highly unusual and, to you, amusing things happen. See the Sources section for information on getting a copy of *Pranks*.

CONCERTS

Ever try to buy tickets to a big concert or other event and get burned by a scalper, promoter, entertainer, or whomever? I bet the universal yes comes from all of us. Of course, there is little you can do about it, except to Hayduke the guilty parties. Our own Andy Cove decided to take this thought the extra step toward delight.

"You could involve your mark in this situation. What if you decided your mark had some tickets available for a popular upcoming concert or sports event? Why not advertise that for him or her?

"You don't need the big money to buy ads in regular media. Just make up cheapo Xerox-copy ads by the dozens and stick them on telephone poles, buildings, and school bulletin boards. Anywhere there is a school or campus this will go down great."

That is Andy's straight idea. He also has some kinks to bend in there, saying, "Suppose you do a few direct-mail ads or personal ones to the 'right people' in which you offer front row or backstage passes in return for perverted sex acts?"

Or, gosh, Andy, take it to the next level and put up public wall ads from your mark offering street drugs, painkillers, and other purloined hospital narcotics, garage-made booze, etc. We could even pimp for his sister.

I can just see Andy's next idea, where Mother Teresa undulates up on the pulpit/stage of the PTL Club, hoists up her habit, and sets her bush on fire.

60

CONDOMS

Wally is a helluva nice guy, one who can get great ideas to help abused women. He told me about a friend of his who wanted to break up a go-nowhere relationship between a kind girl and a sphincter-muscle guy. Wally's pal started to send her gifts in the muscle-mark's name.

"I started out with a few truly tasteless things like truly cheap jewelry, telling her in mash notes how its value reminded me of her. I heard he was really puzzled over it. She wasn't sure she believed his denials because he wasn't all that swift and she wasn't all that cute.

"She saw him as a catch, he saw her as an easy lay."

Wally's pal decided on the quantum gift after an evening in which the muscle mark proved how easy a lay she was and bragged to his jock buddies at the frat.

"I masturbated into a condom, sealed it shut, put a tacky thank-you card on it, and had it delivered to her sorority. It was rough and nasty, but it finally did the trick. This so-called shy girl, to get even with this jerk for what she thought he'd done, started the rumor on campus that he couldn't get it up and that's why she was dropping him."

Don't you just love young romance and justice when it all comes together?

I took some heavy fire from a friend about condom misuse. It was most deserved and right on target. Carla Savage shot me down for suggesting the old hole-in-the-condom stunt in an earlier book. Her major objection must be published.

"While there are a few folks I wouldn't mind killing," Carla says, "I sure as hell would never promote or encourage the kind of mark-related pregnancy that might result from disabling a condom.

"Geez, George, other than the laws of heredity being stacked against us as it is, it is more than enough to have one mark loose in the world without knowingly contributing to the creation of a junior mark or markess."

She's right and I apologize. Perhaps it would be a good idea if all male marks had to have condoms permanently attached to their penii at birth.

As Carla once wisely told me, "Sex is such a great subject. Those who don't get off can always get even." I love that lady!

COPS

There are those days when the bear gets you. It was a day like that when one of my police officer pals walked into our neighborhood gun shop muttering about his partner. He said the guy had the IQ of a throw rug, the personality of a slug, and beyond that, he just didn't like him. One of the resident loafers at the shop had been an MP in another life and proceeded to explain how he dealt with *his* incompetent partner.

"Without going into detail about how often and how messed up he was, just let me say he was too cowardly to stand his ground and too fat to run," the ex-MP said of his former partner. "But one night we got a report of a suspected prowler in the basement of the NCO club.

"I let him follow me a few paces behind as we descended the stairs to the darkened basement. I could hear him wheezing along behind me, his flashlight about as steady as palsy. What he didn't know was that this was a set-up call, made by a pal, who had pulled the circuit-breaker switch so we'd have to use flashlights.

"Meantime, I had moved off to the side of the main room and let him go ahead of me. He got about thirty feet ahead in this big cavernous basement and started to whisper my name. I ducked down behind some boxes, stuck on ear protectors, and tossed a stun grenade simulator out toward the floor.

"He was in shock. My pal and I hustled him out of there and put him back into the Jeep. As he was starting to come out of it, I sat there and asked if he was ready to check out the basement—acting like we'd never been down there and had just arrived. He got all shook up and refused to get out of the vehicle. He took off 'sick' the rest of our shift."

I broke into the monologue to relate how another police officer I knew got back at a cop he had to be associated with at one time. Nobody wanted to ride with this slap-happy Yahoo, so he had a solo car. My friend used to spray tear gas or Mace on the unit's radio microphone or into the heater ducts in the winter. He and other officer put two live chickens in the cop's locker. On his wedding anniversary date they gift wrapped a dead cat, courtesy of the Roadkill Pet Shoppe, put in a card with his name, and had it delivered to his ex-wife.

It's like a bull session here. A lady officer who calls herself Penelope Penophile when we're talking for the record told me a story she heard once about a traffic control cop who told her he got back at assholes who gave him a hard time by doing something really off the wall.

"Nobody ever deserves a moving violation ticket, right? That's the story. So, if a driver really jerks you around, threatens with political juice, stuff like that, this cop I knew would giggle and hold up the guy's license. Then, he'd pop it in his mouth and eat it. No kidding, he'd chew it up and swallow it," she told me.

The citizen would be flabbergasted. Then the cop would tell the guy he was also citing him for driving without a license. "And he'd do it too," she added.

"The best part came at the hearing, usually when the citizen beefed about the officer's actions. This cop, who had the sweetest face, would get on the stand and act all professional and polite about the arrest, then calmly deny everything about eating any license. He'd really patronize the citizen and appeal to the court's dignity as a fellow professional, all the while lying through his teeth. He never lost a bust or a complaint on one. I loved it."

CREDIT CARDS

People in big business make grand use of credit cards. This fact can help you get back at a Mr. or Ms. Big who has done you a rotten turn. Your Mr. or Ms. Big Mark probably has a secretary who screens all incoming calls to see if the caller is Important enough to talk with the bigshot. If so, here's how the telephone conversation should go when you call.

Secretary answers phone and after you ask for Boss says, "And what is the nature of your business with Mr./Ms. Big?"

You respond in a kind of conspiratorial tone, "It's kind of personal, but you see, I am the cleaning lady/man over at the Rooms by the Hour Pussy Cat Motel and I found Mr./Ms. Big's credit card by one of the whore's beds and I wanted to get it back to him."

If the secretary argues, just say you'll mail it to the Big residence.

DAMS

Some very agile and creative EarthFirst!ers from Washington state became some great dam(n) busters by direct-action targeting of the Elwha Dam for an early morning, high-level graffiti attack. These wonderful Haydukers gave the power establishment a major headache with their version of the Washington Water Torture using skill, imagination, courage, and paint.

They painted a large, 100-foot-long black crack down the face of the dam, making it look as if the structure was about to break. They also later painted the legend "ELWHA BE FREE" on the dam's vertical face.

One raider said, "It was the next best thing to really cracking the dam and letting the river's water run free. It was a fun, risky commando raid. We loved it."

The raiders used a combination of rappeling and climbing techniques, no easy feat considering the dam's top is only twenty-four inches wide with no hooks to attach ropes or any gear. Added to that risk is the fact that there are security guards on duty.

Appropriately, the paint they used is labeled "Midnight Black" and it is guaranteed to last ten years. That may be more than you can claim for that dam(n) if someone else gets to it with something stronger than paint.

DOLLARS

The Midnight Avenger uses dollar bills to dispense justice in the form of monetary graffiti. His logic is fine, as he says, "More eyes see paper money than see messy public walls, plus the circulation is far wider. Why not write your nasty payback messages on dollar bills?"

Indeed? Write all sort of offers...drugs, sex, paid killings, political threats, pedophilia, etc., combined with your mark's telephone numbers, work, and home. This is especially fun if the home number is unlisted.

Another possibility with the dollar bill is to deface it. You simply cut out the picture of George Washington and tape in a photo of your mark. Be a big spender—do this for a dozen bills and see that they enter circulation. The next step is to call the Feds about this desecration and/or counterfeiting. But be warned; the Feds take messing with money very seriously, so avoid leaving fingerprints that will finger you instead of your mark.

DOORS

Sure, it was easy back then to lock, nail, or glue Cpl. Guffaw's door shut, causing him to miss formations, meetings, drill, and dozens of other milestones of his daily life. There was a war on and he was a lifer. But my pal Fred Rectal brought this to a new level of fun when he clotheslined his boss's door shut while the beast was shacked up with his secretary. Why was this such a problem, you ask?

"Ahh, you see, I'd called Mrs. Boss and told her I was the boss's assistant, Mr. Mark II, and that she was to come on down and meet her husband at the motel in that little old city thirty-five miles away where he was 'at a sales meeting.' The bimbette was not supposed to be there, of course," Fred explained.

What Fred did was to tie a tough nylon rope to the large doorknob of the room containing the boss and his doxy. He then stretched that rope out and around a sturdy tree some fifteen feet from the door. He snugged that sucker so tight you could have hung one hundred pounds of wet wash on it without a bow.

"Naturally, the door opened inward and when Mr. Boss tried to leave he couldn't get the door open. Naturally, I had already disconnected the phone line in his room so he could not call the desk for help. And it didn't matter; his wife was only about fifteen minutes from arrival and she had the room number."

When Fred saw her arrive and start into the lobby, he cut the rope as she headed up the stairs toward the room. Mr.

Boss had quit trying to tug open the door and was starting to shout for help out of the only window he could open, a small one in the bathroom at the rear of the room.

The next thing Fred reports is the wife knocking on the door and her husband, thinking management had come to rescue him, throwing open the door. Who was most astonished...Mr. Boss? Mrs. Boss? Ms. Bimbette?

Fred was highly amused. So am I.

From time to time it's important to disseminate informational instruction. I refer to Ray Heffer. Ray says if you want to gain entry through a locked door, don't kick it in like you see on TV, unless you're in a helluva noisy hurry.

"Buy a small hydraulic-type jack, those bottle types for small cars, and weld an 18-inch metal extension to the piston rod," Ray says. "An old piece of water pipe will be fine.

"Insert this modified jack sideways between the door frame and the door. Using the pump handle, expand pressure outward to the frame. Expand the pressure more. Obviously, the jack's pressure will spread the door frame to where the door lock will clear the latch plate. The door will open freely."

I tried it. The only sound you hear is a slight creak of splitting wood...ever so slight.

Ray also explains how you can open a locked screen door from the outside without leaving any sign of forced entry. Take a bicycle spoke and grind a tapered point on one end. Insert that end through the screen mesh right under the latch hook. Pull up.

It works. And there is little, if any, trace that the door was tampered with.

DRUGS

Given America's media hysteria over drugs, it's easy to see how this topic has become a wonderful straight man for humorous Haydukery. For instance, former Dodger base-ballers Jay Johnstone and Jerry Reuss used to swipe note-pads from the team doctor and write scary instructions to teammates, e.g., "Due to the presence of abnormality in your recent urine specimen, it is important that you bring me another specimen." Several players fell for it.

Johnstone says that Reuss also conned a couple of team-mates into providing semen samples. Naturally, when the mark walked into the clubhouse he was further victimized by other teammates who had been primed for his arrival by "Dr." Reuss.

Lee Bertoncini had another suggestion. The next time one of your co-workers has to take one of those urine tests, swipe the company doctor's notepad à la Johnstone and write this note: "Due to major abnormality in your recent urine specimen, it is necessary for you to bring in a much larger specimen. Over the next several days will you please fill a quart Mason jar, seal it with the cap, and bring that to my office."

Others who hate this brave new world of the Piss Police have reacted. Sally Boreclay, a noted radical and unforgiving hippie chick, brought her mandatory urine sample to the office in her plant. Her container was filled with apple juice.

Looking at it with a frown, the nurse said, "This surely looks cloudy."

"Not to worry," Sally said with a cackle, "I'll just recycle it for you."

She chugged the apple juice down in one shot, burped, and headed for the ladies room, saying over her shoulder, "Hang in there, Nursey Babe, I'll fill 'er up and be right back."

All of this has to make you wonder: if Nancy Reagan hates dope so much, how comes she's still married to one? That great philosopher, the Rev. Dr. David McGeary, must have been thinking about that, too, when he remarked, "Life is the sentence that man must serve for the sin of being born."

My old pal Doc Sarvis, who is a doctor for real, notes that many dealers now use UPS to transport dope, which seems appropriate because from my dealings with the UPS management, they are dopes. The scam works by purporting to send some illicit substances via UPS and calling the police to report the shipment. You can use this scam to hurt both a primary and a secondary mark.

Doc says the best way is to actually use the real thing, which is an expensive step to take for a scam. Or you can use a lookalike, smellalike, tastealike substitute. Oregano is a good pot substitute. What would work well for coke? Speed? Etc.? Let me hear from you experts.

Keep in mind, however, what one cop told me, that in most states the seriousness of drug crime is in the weight, not the purity. That is, .99 of an ounce of 100% pure cocaine is not as serious a crime as 1+ ounce of 1% cocaine.

DRUNKS

It's not that everyone picks on drunks, it's just that some drunks need to become civilized. We don't appreciate you throwing up on our new sofa, our favorite rug, our car, or our bed. I'm talking here about the bad drunks, people who do evil and unsociable things to other people.

Bummer has a whole menu of goodies to visit upon the dastardly drunks of your life. For example, he suggests spreading some Elmer's glue on a sleeping drunk's body hair. When he or she awakes, the first step will be stiff, followed by a fall. Walking will be hunched and painful.

Want something worse for your drunken mark? Bummer will come through for you. He suggests taking a very ripe, peeled banana and carefully laying it in the crack of the mark's ass. The result will be a soft, mushy buttstain as the mark waddles off to the bathroom in wonderment.

Dental floss makes great bondage wrap for a mark. It won't break easily and usually has to be cut off by someone else. Think about that—new whine in old bottles. Perhaps you can get some bad drunks to take my advice and stop following the liter.

FAN

Ceiling fans are making a major comeback, which is neat. I like them and have ever since I saw my first one in an old Jon Hall South Sea adventure film. In addition to their cooling function, they can be easily converted to Haydukery if you wish to chill a mark. Thanks to Grizzled and some friends of his, we can now offer new insight into that old expression of the shit hitting the fan.

When our friend Grizzled was in high school, he happened to be living in Southeast Asia, where it is a bit muggy. Every classroom had several of these large overhead fans with the wide blades horizontal to the ground.

"We had a nasty trickster who wanted to get back at some of the teachers who had been hassling him for no good reason," he recalled. "He knew they were having a meeting in one of the rooms there, so just after school ended for the day and before the meeting began, he opened several bottles of india ink and placed them upright on the still fan blades. He left the room, waiting for the teachers to come in and sit down and then for someone to switch on the fan."

As Grizzled points out, for maximum results place your open bottle of whatever close to the center axis of the fan so that the whirling force builds up quickly, which will fling the substance further when your little bomb lets go, thanks to centrifugal force.

FARTS

Not all marks are horrible individuals deserving to get your best or worst shot right in their soft ego. Not every mark is someone plotting to overthrow God's Own America or kidnap blue-eyed Christian babies for the purposes of ritual cult murders with possible cannibalistic overtones. No, sometimes your mark is just simply society as a whole, with or without the "w" in front.

For such times as you just feel like Hayduking the world, Uncle Gerry and Rusty suggest you turn to your trusty CB radio, saying, "We love it when some old neighborhood biddies are gossiping away on the CB. We have a way of blowing them away and getting some good air time and some laughs at the same time.

"Both Uncle Gerry and I work up these great, huge farts — enough gas to float three dirigibles, you know. Then we turn on the CB to their channel and one right after the other we blow these farts at the old biddies."

To get the full impact of this, you need to witness a Big Fart Attack by this disgorging duo. I have personally witnessed Uncle Gerry blast paint off the wall of a room three houses away from the fart scene. He also once blew an ass-full of rectal suppositories through a 3/8-inch plywood board.

If that's not enough for you, can you imagine the result if every single person in the world farted at the exact same time?

OK, you're not laughing. As my publisher once pointed

out to me, "You know, George, not everyone is as amused by farting and belching as you are." No, I really don't know. Let's find out. Let's take a poll. If you, gentle reader, are amused or not amused by gastronomic eructation and flatulence, (aka belching and farting), please address a postal card to Fart Poll, c/o George Hayduke, P.O. Box 1307, Boulder, CO 80306.

I will report the results in the next book and will award a prize to the reader who comes up with the best reason for or against fart/belch stories in my books. Decision of the judges will be final.

Which reminds me of a court case which was actually reported in the *Chicago Tribune*. Isn't that the home base of my favorite fan in newspaper journalism, Gutsy Bob Greene? Anyway, if the pro-farters win the poll I'll tell the story next time out.

FIREE

Unruly, irate, unfair, and sleazy bosses are common bullies whose underhanded deeds against fair, loving, or at least loyal employees come through the Hayduke Hotline daily. Sometimes, though, we look through the wrong end of the telescope in viewing this problem, i.e., there are some really terrible employees, too.

While talking to some nice people from the Cincinnati area on WLW radio, I got a call from Joe, an employer. He told about some rotten employees who lied, cheated, stole, and otherwise gave him a bad time. It was a mirror image horror story. Joe had a solution, all for entertainment purposes only, of course.

"When I have to fire a really evil person who's cost me a lot," Joe told us, "I use the IRS to help pay them back for their unfair, costly personal and financial expense to me. I simply add some 'money' to their gross income on their annual W2 form that I report to the local, state, and federal governments. You know, I just add some extra digits to their reported income. Of course they never saw any of that money. Let them hassle it out with the IRS."

Joe reported that only once did this bounce back to his court and he shrugged and told the IRS that he'd had an incompetent bookkeeper who must have made the error. They said OK and went away.

"The thing is to keep the amount reasonable enough to seem legitimate," Joe added.

FLASHPAPER

This is a gimmick trick, but thanks to the Midnight Avenger it will work. The basic is flashpaper, available from any magic supply house in most large cities. The stuff is great—it bursts into flashing fire—very spectacular. You can store bundles of it in potentially hot places belonging to your mark, like fireplaces, car engines, cigars, or lamps.

Can you see adding this to the kindling laid nicely for a fire by your mark? Can you see lining an oven bed with it? Can you see arming your mark with flashpaper as a fire-starter? Can you imagine substituting flashpaper for your mark's marriage license, graduation certificate, etc.?

FOOD

Food is fun stuff, even if you can't eat it because it tastes awful. But I'm getting ahead of Bill Hurley. According to Uncle Gerry and Rusty, life is very uncertain so you'd better eat your dessert first. Bill Hurley does that and more.

An accomplished masticator, Bill Hurley knows how to gross out the mark(s) with whom he dines. If he wishes to put his sustenance scenario into play, he digs in with relish.

"I look right at the mark(s) and put large bites of whatever we're eating into my mouth. I chew with gusto and noise, trying to keep my mouth open part of the time. Sometimes smaller pieces of food fall out. But that doesn't spoil my performance," Bill relates.

Bill stops chewing, then deliberately begins to spit his chewed food back out onto his plate. He plays with it. Holds it up to the light, examines it, maybe rolls it into balls or chunks. He gooshes different chewed bits together.

"Then I start to pick up these little piles and pop 'em back into my mouth to eat again, noisily and with gusto. I do this, of course, only after offering the plate to my fellow diners who are my marks."

Don Silverman of WJNO in Florida is my kind of talk show host in that he too fights for the little guy against the bullying institutions. Don knows this restaurant that does not have the friendliest or cleanest waitpersons in the land. He says the place should be renamed Surlyland.

"I got in a hassle with the manager over some of the salad bar offerings being a bit mature. For example, the lettuce was beyond limp, it was in terminal decay. The tomatoes were a sickly orange and dimpled with liver spots. All I got for my mild complaint was a 'So, don't eat here' from this dog of a manager," Don explained to me.

While Don took the manager's advice, he did return to the scene of the insult, but not to eat. He says, "I knew the type of plates and dishes they used and snuck one of my own like theirs into the salad bar line. I had scooped some Alpo into the dish and simply placed it on the salad bar line."

You, of course, may wish to substitute some other ingredients of your own. It's the thought that counts in a tasteful stunt like Don's.

FUSES

A very easygoing teddy bear, Pepper once worked for a horrible boss who used to bully employee's personal lives. This boss once ordered Pepper to watch his home and water his lawn while he was away.

"I did it because I'm a nice guy. But I also made sure I could have access to his home should he become more intolerable at work. He did and I did," Pepper said.

Pepper lived in an old house with old wiring. Fuses frequently blew, so Pepper had a supply of blown fuses of the type also used in the boss's home.

"While the boss was away for a summer week-long business trip, I went in and opened his freezer door to get as quick a defrost as possible. I replaced the perfectly good fuse for the freezer with one of my burned-out ones. I left the door open for five days. The odor was getting rank. I closed the freezer door the day before he was due home."

The nasty boss found that apparently a fuse had blown and that nearly $800 worth of meat had spoiled. He could hardly blame the employee he'd ordered to watch the house and water the lawn because he hadn't given Pepper a key. He was frustrated, furious, and shouted all over the office about his own house wiring.

"The jerk even paid an electrician $75 to come in and check everything, then gave him hell when he didn't find anything and couldn't tell him why the fuse had blown. I plan to continue my efforts to make this man more civilized," Pepper added.

GAS STATIONS

Ahh, back to the scene of so much unhappiness. Before he joined the Navy, Pusgley was a pump jockey in the Carolinas. One thing that soured him on civilian avarice was that his boss cheated old people who came to the station for gas.

"When we devised a self-serve island I got my mind busy with revenge ideas. It was amazing how easily this one came to me," Pusgley related.

The plan hinged on the fact that a lot of older folks make mistakes and try to get the cheaper leaded gasoline into their cars rather than the unleaded variety.

"I called the state regulatory agency and told them the station owner was actively encouraging people to do this. I also told them he had a special funnel out there so anyone could pump leaded fuel into the car's unleaded gas filler opening," Pusgley said.

After two calls, agents showed up to stake out the station. Sure enough, some seniors did their own pumping and Pusgley had thoughtfully supplied a large funnel for others to use in the likely event the leaded pump nozzle wouldn't fit in their filler.

Not only did the station owner get nailed, but the stupid bureaucratic agents also hassled the senior citizens and even arrested two of them. One was the 70-year-old former mayor of the community who wasn't even involved in the gas pumping but was just hanging out at the station.

The black-eye punch publicity to the station owner and to

the police was well worth the time and phone call energy invested.

GAYS

Gay people take a lot of undeserved shit from people whose main contribution to evolution is that they don't walk on all fours because of peer pressure. From the get-go, I like a lot of gay folks. I have gay friends, just as I have other friends who tend to piss off "normal" people and frighten grown-ups of all ages. Don't get on my case for gay bashing.

Roy Blount, a delightful raconteur, spoke for me as well when he said, "I have been around gay couples who seem a lot better matched than I have been with several women."

One of the finest sights I saw during that Gay Rights parade in Phoenix was a young, athletic-looking guy carrying a sign that read "I AM YOUR WORST FEAR AND YOUR BEST FANTASY." True for anyone or not, it made me laugh.

Anyway, a fan we'll call Mr. Lupero is a retired government employee who is gay. Mr. Lupero once had a very bad business dealing with a retired military man—we'll call him Hal Johnson—who later found out that our pal was gay and went out of his way to be a meanass about it. He tried to destroy Mr. Lupero's otherwise well-earned reputation in the community.

Instead of making a big fuss, Mr. Lupero simply wrote a very sweet and sexually explicit letter to the chapter president of the local Pagan Motorcycle Club. His letter was from Hal Johnson, of course, who was scared witless when a horde of irate bikers invaded his home.

"Eventually, the police were called by neighbors and on

83

the surface got things sorted out," Mr. Lupero told me, "but to both the police and the bikers, Hal Johnson was now branded as an aggressively active homosexual who lied about it. How fitting."

GRAFFITI

Once more the scrawl of the wild beckons and we move to the word war of the walls, where paint or pen is at least more legible than the sword. These graffiti are credited if I know the source. Otherwise, they're just here, bared for your use like literary fangs.

If a few literary critics wonder what is the difference between this section and Insults, it is that these messages, usually more terse, came directly from actual graffiti sightings. We must remain true to pure science, even if it is only social, yawn, science.

- BETTER A SOFT, WET DORK THAN A HARD ASS BORK
- SUBVERT PROGRESS
- DAMN THE FEDS, NOT OUR RIVERS
- JUST ANOTHER MORMON ON DRUGS
- AMERICAN FREEDOM: LOVE IT OR LEAVE US ALONE (antigovernment message in federal building, New Orleans)
- I BRAKE FOR BIG TITS! (bumper sticker spotted by Uncle Gerry, without Rusty, in Punta Gorda, FL)

HORSES

No, this isn't about heroin. It's from Kansas City's Ray Heffer and it's his telling of a good old American Indian prank that you can use to pay back one of your marks or markesses who happens to ride horses. It's a simple trick of nature; just find a couple of good-sized cockleburs and stick them to the underside wool skirt liner of the horse's saddle.

Ray guarantees that when the mark or markess mounts up and plops down on that bur-loaded part of the saddle, he or she will start a wild ride, although it may not be a long one.

HUNTERS

Up front, let me say that usually I'm on the side of the animals in these disputes, unless it involves radical animal rights jerks like Cleveland Amory and others of that ilk. On the other hand, I'm also less than fond of the orange-safety-necked hunter radicals.

Tennessee wildlife officers used a trick I suggested some books ago to catch poachers and slob hunters who shoot from their vehicles. They placed decoy deer, either stuffed ones or freshly roadkilled bodies, in spots they could use as ambush points to arrest the bad guys. Along comes a piggy-lazy shooter who takes a shot or two at the decoy. Boom, the wildlife police arrest the guy. Neat.

I was thinking about taking it a shot or two further. What if you made a lifelike dummy of another hunter or farmer and placed it in a field or woods? Place ID on it in the name of your mark. Wait until you see some other hunters or some neighbors coming by and shoot the decoy dummy. Run like hell to your car, then drive away. The "witnesses" won't know what to make of all of this but I bet they call the authorities. They'll know, and, eventually, so will your mark. That's when the mental abuse will start, i.e., "Can you think of anyone who would want to shoot you, Mr. Mark?"

INSULTS

This section is a collection of one-liners, insults, head-turners, nauseating humor, and other bon mots you can toss contemptuously at your various marks. These little gems always work best when used at full volume and in full public. The goal is embarrassment or even, oh joy to achieve, outrage on the part of the mark. In some of the examples you will note a blank line. You are to fill in the appropriate name, religion, political party, gender, ethnic or racial persuasion, etc. of the mark.

- Do you know the difference between a _____ and a toilet seat? A toilet seat doesn't follow you around for two weeks after you've used it.
- You know, it's a good thing_____ and _____ married each other. That way only two people are sickly miserable instead of four.
- My God! That was a helluva fart! (THIS HAS TO BE SHOUTED)
- If a skunk and _____were both run over on the highway, there would be skid marks in front of the skunk.
- Your spouse/lover looks like raw ape puke.
- But it's illegal to sell street drugs! (SAID LOUDLY IN PUBLIC)

IRS

To be sure, owing money to a Mafia loan shark is probably dangerously worse than owing it to the IRS sharks. But the fed enforcers can also get downright nasty trying to collect what they feel is Uncle's share of your earnings. Unlike the Mob collectors, I don't think the IRS has deliberately killed anyone...yet.

Despite this bitch of a reputation, the IRS is a magnificent tool in the Hayduker's arsenal. The threat of IRS interest in his finances could make your mark feel like his ass was put on sideways and he had to take a dump real bad.

Chris D. in Cleveland says to call your mark at work, about 4:30 on a Friday afternoon, especially if the following Monday is to be one of myriad federal holidays. Tell the mark you are from the IRS and demand that the mark be at the IRS regional office in the federal building on Monday or Tuesday, the next business day. If that office is in a city some miles from the mark's home, so much the better.

The mark is told to report at 7:30 A.M. with all his records for the past year. He may bring his accountant and/or attorney if he wishes. When the mark begins to stammer for some information or explanation, you or your associate explains very politely, firmly, and formally that you are sorry, you cannot discuss this matter on the telephone. That is what the meeting is about.

The mark will sweat the entire two or three days of that weekend, calling friends, associates, legal advice, etc. The mark will not be able to call IRS officials because they aren't in the office. The mark sweats some more.

The secondary fun occurs when the mark and his entourage report as ordered. Perhaps some tertiary humor will be realized if the IRS people, a paranoid and suspicious lot, grow curious about the mark, his fear, and this alleged prank.

This one left me weak with laughter, too weak to fart, even after a baked bean dinner. Seriously, the IRS ought to use as its new service motto: DEDICATED TO HANDICAPPING THE HIRED.

Before sharing his holy writ with me, the Silent Samaritan noted that of all the professions and industries, collecting taxes and selling Jesus were probably the most profitable. Not being one to argue with truth, I examined his thought for a mark who had turned a rabidly nasty lawyer upon Samaritan.

"It was hardly worth any challenge. I just got some copies of IRS Form 1099 (a claim form used for extra sources of income) and filled them out in the mark's name, then added some figures of my own as coming from a secondary mark. I sent this to the IRS with proper letters in forged letterhead. Little did they know as they passed along this economic virus.

"Of course, all of this showed up in the proper envelopes at the proper tax time for my mark to panic over."

JUNK MAIL

John Raymond, a writer for the *Atlanta Constitution*, once explained his own rules for dealing with mail, advising, "If it's not a personal letter or a check...throw it out." While I personally believe you must pay your obligated bills, too, I would apply his rule to the daily effluvia of advertising we get flushed into our mail receptacles.

It's not justified, and thanks to Letterman (no, not that one; this one knows the United States Postal Service well), we are paying for this commercial insult more than we know. Junk mail does *not* subsidize first-class mail, it's the other way around.

"According to USPS figures, first-class mail is 54.5% of all mail, bringing in 61.2% of the money. Junk mail is 32.3% of the volume and brings in only 14.7% of the revenue. Junk mail brings in only about one-third the revenue of first-class mail," Letterman told me.

Now, folks—low, sinister giggle here—what does that suggest to you?

What it suggests to the Armchair Avenger is that junk mailers and their willing agents of delivery, the U.S. Postal Service, must be taught some expensive lessons. He says, "Junk mailers pay only 20 percent of the cost you pay to send fliers. They also deduct this business postage off their income tax. We subsidize their advertising shit by paying higher and higher postal charges ourselves. *Enough!!*"

Here is what he proposes. Remove the address label from your unwanted mail. Using a rubber stamp and red ink,

91

stamp the legend UNSOLICITED MAIL—RETURN TO SENDER where the label was. Redeposit all and any such mail in a nearby postal box and let the USPS, its employees, and the junk mailers worry about it.

Because there is no mailing label on the piece it will either have to be returned to the sender, which costs him money, or it will have to be stored or destroyed, which costs the USPS time and energy. Maybe someone will get the point after a while.

Think of the statistics. If 100 million of us dumped five junk mail pieces a day back into the system that would be 500 million pieces of trashed mail someone would have to do something with. I love it. But wait, there's more.

Mr. Avenger has another idea, but this one is very illegal, so he says it is for theoretical entertainment purposes only. That means you shouldn't laugh too hard, I guess.

Go to a *very* trusted printer you know and order several hundred or several thousand *exact* copies of some postage-paid return envelopes from your least favorite junk mailer. You can then use these to send porno, bricks, other messages, competitor's advertising, etc., back to the advertiser. Evil, isn't it? He has to pay all the postal charges on these returns. This stunt is illegal and dangerous, so be careful of fingerprints and other errors.

Finally, the Armchair Avenger says you can screw up the USPS automated scanning machines by altering the bar code that usually appears at the bottom of the postage-paid return envelopes. Try using a Magic Marker of the same color as the bar code to extend the length of some of the shorter bars, messing up the system and causing either errors or stoppage.

There is another side to this argument and I am not referring to the junk mailers. Those buzzards have no argument. This argument comes from lonely and/or curious people who actually like to receive junk mail. Yes, I have heard from a few of them. To help them, or to provide you others with a never-ending source of junk mail to send your mark, please say thanks to Mr. Urban Resistance Fighter, who informed me about an outfit that guarantees to "get you enough junk mail delivered to last well into the twenty-first century." According to Urban Resistance Fighter, they are as follows:

National Junk Mail Directory
P.O. Box 7777-Y
New York, NY 10116

He also notes that you must sign a statement that you are over twenty-one years of age.

LAUNCHER

Need something to launch projectiles such as water, paint, or stink-filled balloons at your mark or his building? Freddie the Fez comes through with his three-person launcher, aka Freddie's Surgical Tube Catapult. Freddie says to get some surgical tubing, i.e., latex rubber hose from a medical supply shop. You also need one of those plastic baskets of the sort used at fast food places to serve fries.

The launcher requires two people to hold the tubing over their heads with the other ends attached to the plastic burger basket. The firer places one or two balloons filled with whatever disgusting ingredients you can stomach putting in them into the basket.

Each party stretches his element with as much tension as possible. The firer aims the projectiles and releases the basket. Freddie claims accurate and very messily devastating hits at well over one hundred meters.

He adds, "We used pop, corn sugar syrup, motor oil, paint, urine, thinned tar, diarrhea, vomit, and worse to fill our balloons."

Ol' Soot 'n Ink also describes a launcher he invented, calling it the Funnelator. It is basically a long-range, high-payload delivery system. Here are Soot 'n Ink's instructions for building your own model Funnelator.

Get a large (minimum ten inches) zinc-plated funnel from your local farm supply store. Make sure it is (1) good U.S. steel and (2) sturdy.

Mount a firing handle by running a long carriage bolt

94

through a large washer from inside the funnel, so it won't pull through the spout from the inside. Then run that bolt through a one-inch hardwood dowel crosswise to the spout. The dowel is now attached to the bottom of the spout by the bolt and washer coming from inside the funnel and secured by a nut at the dowel end. Tighten.

Next, attach two S hooks at the rim and on either side of the funnel. Line up the hooks with the projecting ends of the dowel. Attach a pair of bicycle inner tubes to the S hooks.

You mount the hooks on the Y fork of a large tree, a metal brace, poles stuck in the ground, a door frame, in a pickup truck's stake bed, or wherever you wish to fire from.

According to Soot 'n Ink, you must see this super slingshot in action to believe its power, range, and accuracy. His list of favored projectiles includes runny excrement loaded in old bread bags, dead animals, pint-sized Ziploc bags loaded with paint, roofing tar wrapped in wax paper, rotten cantaloupes, and small watermelons.

He adds some war stories, too, noting, "One time I had a terrible boss whose dog got hit by a car while she was at work. I got to her dog first and took the body home with me. She never knew it was dead, and thought it had run away for the day.

"I put a tiny hangman's noose around its neck, then loaded it into my portable Funnelator mounted on my truck bed after driving late at night to within two hundred feet of her home.

"George, you would not believe the loud, smashing sound that her dead dog made when it was projected at high speed into an aluminum-sided house. At work the next day, she tearfully told some other bosses that her little doggy had 'come all undone' from the impact. Isn't that neat?"

Ol' Soot 'n Ink tells us to practice a lot for accuracy and speed of attack/disengagement. He recommends a crew of three—a loader, firer, and driver—for the mobile hits.

LAWNS

Ms. Penelope Kishkas is proud of her lawn. She is also quite a gunlady, as she proved to Grizzled when she blew away his best friend, a nice old dog, that happened to only tread, not poop, on her premises. Grizzled is a kindly, patient man, and he waited until the following spring to get partially back at this murderous mama.

"Her lawn is immaculate, but it's also well lighted. I solved that problem with projectiles," Grizzled explains. "I filled some balloons with a mixture of old motor oil and a strong commercial defoliant, then launched them on her yard late at night in a hit 'n run raid."

He reports the combination did the trick in about a week, showing off four "bomb craters" of dead grass scattered in her former oasis of a lawn.

Rapid Revenge works for a landscape engineer and tells me that if you're truly unhappy enough with a mark to go after the lawn, you need to use a product like Round Up. Spraying it on the mark's lawn will murder the grass totally. Rapid says it costs major bucks to replace the lawn, as well.

MACE

You can buy commercial containers of CS and other military/law enforcement irritant gases. Or you can use the suggestion of Bryan S. and Rob M. to make your own version of Mace.

Mix three parts alcohol, one-half part iodine, and one-half part salt. They tell me you can also use three parts alcohol and one part iodized salt. The guys say it is a fine Mace substitute and really does a number on the mark's eyes and breathing.

Delivery systems could include a small atomizer or a fill-it-yourself spray can available at hardware stores. Be careful of firing this stuff into shifting winds, however.

MAGIC

Being a professional stage magician, Jim Helik of Toronto told me how very useful many items sold in magician's shops (*not* the usual mall-variety gag/joke shop) would be to someone in my line of work. There is usually such a shop in many major cities, and after you convince the owner that you are a professional magician you can buy useful items.

Some of the ones Jim suggested as basic include flash powder, flashpaper, and a useful fire powder known as Dragon's Breath. He also recommends hand flashers, a hand-held firing device, Dissolvo paper, a paper that totally dissolves in tap water, trick handcuffs, lock picks, straitjackets, instructional books on stunts, etc.

Jim also suggests shopping at theatrical supply houses. Again, the secret is to convince the shop clerk or owner that you're a pro. Perhaps a few phony press clippings, ID card, or business card would help, as would tossing around the proper jargon.

MARBLES

The next time someone asks you what possible use marbles have, those hard glass balls that we kids from so many generations ago used to play with, tell them to see Neal in Atlanta. Neal had a roommate who used to borrow stuff from his medicine cabinet all the time and never stocked her own. As Neal says, "It was cheaper and easier for her to rob my cabinet than to buy her own. That's where my marble collection, all six hundred of them, came in."

Using a piece of cardboard as a dam, Neal very carefully filled his roommate's cabinet with marbles, hundreds of the hard little spheres. He then closed the door and removed the cardboard. Later that night, he heard her open his cabinet, get what she wanted, then open her cabinet. The next sound was a combination of rolling clatter, a very loud scream, followed by some unladylike curses.

I regret I have no report of the long-term effect of this stunt upon the mark.

MESS

This one is so delightfully awful that I chose the generic name of "Mess" to adequately describe its purpose in your life. It is a delight when used in cars, homes, apartments, offices, stores—almost anywhere you wish to create, well, a mess.

The "it" is an Air Texture Gun, an electrically powered tool nominally used by contractors for interior decoration and renovation. I see no reason why you can't use this remarkable device for the same purpose on something owned by your mark.

You have this mark who's the kind of dickhead who would celebrate Pearl Harbor Day by throwing a sushi party at Benihana. He or she has a really lovely car, home, office, or whatever, of which she or he is very proud and keeps very, very neat. This pride borders on obsession. This mark has done something evil to you. You know about the obsession. You now also know about the Air Texture Gun, which can spray joint cement, texture compound, paint, splatter, gooey plaster, oil, gunk, or just about any mess you want to use onto ceilings, walls, floors, windows, drapes, furniture, artwork, etc.

These fun guns are available at any and all building supply houses, discount stores, and through the mail. They are great tools. I know.

MONEY

When I tried work as a business cog some years ago, I heard the axiom that "A Dollar is What You Label It." I now know where that bromide originated—with Midwestern Will. His is a novel use for paper money that brings true meaning to the term "marked money."

Will suggests putting your mark's name, address, telephone number, Social Security number, charge card numbers, etc., on paper money. List this data about your mark on all the bills of all denominations. The following wonderful occurrences may happen:

1. Some graduates of the Hayduke School of Mayhem might come in contact with the marked money and practice what the master would teach.

2. Some credit scam criminals could easily come across some of these bills and acquire a new mark of their own.

3. Other transgressors who specialized in burglary might note these specialized bills and realize a new customer.

4. The FBI or IRS might be curious about this money.

5. Will bets that the Treasury Department has regulations about marking or defacing money. They do. Why not send them a few samples as an investment in creative justice.

Again, heed the warning in the Dollars section about leaving incriminating fingerprints on the bills.

MONKEY SHIT

All you shop guys and mechanics recognized this one right off as Babbit-Rite. It is an industrial putty known to many users as "monkey shit," which it resembles when it gets a mite dirty. Our friend Jimmy Carter suggests combining Babbit-Rite with other chemicals, especially odor-causing ones, to create real look-alike/smell-alike ca ca. The stuff can be molded to any shape and will adhere to most surfaces.

The applications of this compound are endless and amusing. It is readily available from industrial supply stores.

MOTEL

Old Pepper's back off the road again and he's got a story about how he paid back Motel Hell for making his home away from home a very bad scene. Pepper says, "I won't bore you with details, other than rude, waddling waitresses, food I wouldn't feed to a starving Contra, a dirty room with a broken TV, and a bed that must have been used once as a landing pad for flying elephants."

Pepper did a few get-backs and will share some of the nicer ones with you. Because his room key was apparently a master for his wing of the motel, he was able to get into seven other rooms, all empty. Here's what he did.

- He carefully unwrapped soap, placed pubic hair on the bars, and resealed the soap package.
- He altered the checkout times on the room cards, making it read 4 P.M. rather than noon.
- In some of the rooms he jam-stuck the thermostat on high heat, while in others he put it on cold air-conditioning.
- In one Gideon Bible, Pepper put porno pictures, while in another he left the name and phone number of a nasty ex-sweetie who lived in the city.

As Pepper said, "All in all, I think everything balanced out for all parties. In any case, I haven't heard anything about it in the past year and I never returned."

NAPALM

Several hand-wringing worriers were all whined out because I gave you folks a formula for napalm in the last book. I wonder how they feel about Du Pont, which made the stuff I saw dumped on real people...but I digress.

For those of you who don't own even bathroom chemistry experience and don't or won't make napalm because of its reputation, I offer an alternative—a paraffin/sawdust incendiary device. It's almost as effective as napalm, though it requires more boost to start it going. Also, it is solid state when cool and more stable than napalm, thus, safer.

All you need is dry sawdust and paraffin (or candle wax). You melt the paraffin and stir in about the same volume of sawdust. Stir until it cools and starts going to a solid state. Remove the mixture from your container and let it cool completely. It will become solid.

Use fist-sized lumps for your actions. You can easily transport these in a paper sack. Any sort of fire-oriented ignition system will do the job.

OLIVER NORTH

I'll bet that name made you sit up a bit taller and got your mind running a bit more deviously. Speaking of whom, do you know why the sun never really set on Ollie's Empire? It's because God would never trust a Reaganista in the dark. Actually, Fred Rexer told me that joke.

Anyway, at the height of the Iran/Contra hoopla, when Olliemania replaced Wrestlemania as Muddle America's drug of choice, all sorts of patriotic opportunists were avariciously trying to make money by selling Ollie shirts, bumper stickers, masks, pictures, coffee mugs, and even The Man himself to be our new Commander in Chief. This gave R. Ken Brown an idea.

"All these peckerhead rednecks were running ads in *Shotgun News* selling Ollie North junk. I had an enemy who was a staunch right-wing America-first kind of guy who suspected that even General Singlaub was a KGB disinformation agent. He thought minorities were put on this earth for target practice. What a way to make his day!"

You're aware of the flip side of Olliemania, i.e., the HATE THE RAGHEADS industry with its paper firing-range targets featuring pictures of Khomeini, Ortega, Khadaffi, Castro, etc. Our hero, Kenny, put the two together and made a Hayduke sandwich with his mark in the middle.

"I ran this wonderfully illustrated ad in some of the more virulent right-wing publications showing a firing-range target of Ollie. My ad copy was a satire of the usual Third World bashing done by the nuts on the Right—the 'set your

105

sights on Ollie' kind of thing. I used my enemy/mark's name and address for the logo. Several friends in the cities where the publications were located took in the ad copy and the cash.

"The ads ran, then the calls and hate mail started pouring in, both to the publications and to my mark. He has everyone furious with him and nobody believes it was a set up. You know how simple-minded and paranoid they are," Kenny said with a howl of laughter.

Wow, I bet his mark must still feel like he's surrounded by diarrhetic elephants.

PANTIES

Child molestation is a cruel and barbaric fact of life. The fact that the sight of a little girl gets some psychopaths hornier than a zoo monkey is very useful knowledge for you. As the official philosopher of the Grubbtown/Blairsville Bus Company, a new wave heavy metal group, Lee has put this to work for her.

"This mark had done some rotten things to me and I couldn't get relief through work because of the usual old-boys network. I couldn't afford an attorney, either," Lee related.

"But I could afford to buy little girl's panties and did so," Lee said. "I got some cute little panties with flowers and little animals on them. I started to place these in my mark's office, on the door to his office, in his mailbox, and even stuffed panties in his briefcase."

Said Lee, "It got the guy in a lot of hassle at home, started rumors at work, and he was even called upstairs to explain what in the hell was going on. He couldn't, of course, which is why this stunt was so great."

Lee added that she was always very civil, correct, positive, and innocent around the mark, giving him no reason to suspect her of being the cause of his problems.

PARTIES

Did you ever go to one of those parties where you were so bored that you began to wonder why you were there and suddenly realized that if you knew the answer you'd be bored even more? Or do you owe a payback to some evil host or hostess for some past nasty done to you? Hark, Dr. Roy Infinger, county coroner for Eremite County, Utah, has a suggestion.

He takes a supply of hazelnuts and removes the tops very carefully with a very sharp instrument. He extracts the nut from the shell and inserts a colorful condom in its place. Then he carefully reseals the top back into the shell with plastic wood and/or super glue.

I've seen his finished product and unless you are looking specifically for the doctored item you can't distinguish it from an undoctored one, so to speak.

Our good doctor fills his pockets with these little treasures and goes to his social function target. If there is a bowl of unshelled nuts on one of the side tables, and there usually is in his society, he simply places some of his Doctor's doctored nuts in with the others and goes about the party, being careful to observe the action.

It's usually only a short time until some soul happens along and makes use of the nutcracker and some of the nuts. Obviously, when one of the rubber-filled nuts is discovered, it is greeted by reactions ranging from embarrassed sobs to screams to cackles of silly delight. Nearly always, the reaction attracts the attention of those nearby, which always attracts the hostess or host. By the time the little treasure inside the shell has been unrolled, the secondary mark has attracted quite an audience, most of whom are paying more curious attention to the primary mark or markette (the host).

Several refinements are possible here, according to the good Doctor Infinger, including making a local market your mark. You can even fill the condom with mayonnaise before inserting it into the shell and mix food coloring in with the mayonnaise.

PAWNSHOP

As all of us will, Dr. Deviant got down on his luck, was between jobs, and needed some money to keep his life moving ahead. He decided, most reluctantly, to pawn his good 35mm camera and zoom telephoto lens. Dressed neatly and being very polite, the Doctor entered a local pawnshop and explained his plight.

The owner obviously mistook him for a street scum and started to scream at him to get out of his shop. He swore at the Doctor, called him a common criminal, and shouted that he didn't buy stolen cameras.

"I had never even been in a pawnshop before, let alone a police station. I was stunned," Dr. Deviant explained. "I tried to talk nicely to him and to offer proof that it was my camera. He threatened to call the police. I left his shop. But as I was walking away, I began to think that calling the authorities into the matter was a very good idea."

Dr. Deviant went to a trusted printer in another town and had a bunch of advertising leaflets printed in the name of the pawnshop and its owner. He advertised cheap handguns, switchblade knives, silencer kits, parts for machine guns, and special-effect sexual equipment. These leaflets were stuck on cars in the local shopping center that next Saturday morning. As fortune would have it, police, both local and national, visited the pawnshop that same afternoon.

PHOTO SHOP

In addition to being a nice guy and a solidly nonviolent contributor to Haydukery, The Hat is a photo fan. Naturally, he was dismayed when his trusty old Rolleiflex broke down and needed to be repaired. I'll spare you the details, which aren't happy ones, but to be brief, the camera store management really screwed Hat and returned his camera in even worse condition than when he brought it in for repair. He got no satisfaction from the usual Golden Rule and Chamber of Commerce methods.

"I waited nearly a year, then set out to get even," says The Hat. "I had three thousand fliers printed with the store's name, logo, hours, etc., including coupons for free film, free processing, and 30 percent discounts on all other services. I spread these all over town, including the malls.

"For my second attack I had three hundred bumper stickers printed in garish Day-Glo colors (your book covers inspired me, George). They read "I ♥ JERK'S CAMERA SHOP," only I used the real shop name and address.

"I picked out really expensive cars I'd see in town, like BMW, Mercedes, Ferrari, Rolls, Maserati, etc., and stuck one of these ugly stickers on the rear deck of each car.

"My final assault was to take out an ad in our local shopper newspaper to announce a PHOTO FAIR PARTY at the home of the owner of the camera shop and invite the entire community to come over and get acquainted. I announced free food and drink, and wrote that manufacturer's reps would be there with free equipment and supplies, there would be sexy models, etc."

The Hat also made copies of this ad and plastered them all over the local campus. The ad ran only the day before the party so there'd be no time to run any correction. He also had announcements made on the local radio station—all charged to the camera shop, of course.

The Hat reports that all phases were great successes. In Phase One, the mark was forced to give away great amounts of supplies and services to avoid police and the courts. He was also billed for all of the printing The Hat had done. In Phase Two, he had to pay damages to several of the car owners and was actually taken to court by two of them. Finally, the party turned into a near riot and the police had to be called.

PHOTOGRAPHY

This idea comes from V.P. Kowalski, with inspiration from Eastman Kodak, a narrow-minded company that got some fun-seeking amateur in trouble with the Reagan Bedroom Gestapo at both the Post Office and Justice Department. The man had sent film to Kodak with nude photos on it. The bluenoses passed moral judgment about what they considered off-color about someone else's pictures. They confiscated the film and called the cops.

Anyway, when I'm done explaining V.P. Kowalski's scam, we'll put our minds to paying back Kodak. Brother Kowalski says to go to some store and buy a prepaid processing mailer. Guess whose brand we suggest using?

Load your camera. Get some hard-core porno at an adult store. Put a macro-zoom lens on your 35mm and copy the porn pictures. Use care to crop the edges and to focus out the halftone dots on the printed pictures. Of course, if you can get willing and cooperating live models, that would be so much more fun. However...

Put your mark's spouse's name and address on the mailer, insert the film, and send this little photo bomb on its way to the target. You get a major direct hit whether the company calls the cops or returns the completed pictures.

Now, about Eastman Kodak. What's that? Oh, right. Never mind.

POOP

Jordan Smythe, a regular at the Messy Stool Bar in Salmon, likes to tell this one on himself. He was driving along one night so drunk he couldn't pronounce it and badly needed to defecate...very badly.

"I was hurrying to get home as my bowels were about to move on their own. Without looking, I quickly pulled over to the other side of the road and parked on the wide shoulder there. I had not seen the cop until he parked behind me, his lights rolling red and blue.

"He asked me what I was doing over on the wrong side of the road. I told him I had to take a dump. He told me I was drunk. Insulted, I cocked my leg and did a loud, messy dump right in my pants, right there in my car.

"The officer seemed to be very upset. He ordered me out of my truck and to clean myself up, that I was under arrest. He was growing livid. I had a roll of paper towels and cleaned myself up somewhat, throwing my shitty pants in the back of my truck. I finished my wipe job, then slid my messy ass across his seat, obeying his order to get in the car. He grew even more livid. He made me clean off his seat.

"He then took my towels and spread them on the seat of his car before I got in, under arrest for drunk driving and for defecating in public. I was a real hit at the police station and the other cops ripped all over the arresting officer for bringing me in. I was jailed and the DUI stuck."

So what's the joke, the punch line, the grabber? Let Jordan continue.

114

"The joke on them was that I was holding at the time of my arrest. I had a baggie full of some very fine weed in my pants pocket, some real primo Noriega marijuana. The next day I went back out to my truck and sure enough, there was my stash. Who's gonna dig around in shit-covered pants?"

Gnarly likes the holiday season except for the thieves who prey on the sick, the elderly, and the poor folks who can't fend for themselves. You know, those nasty Dirtballs who rip off or vandalize mail, presents, lawn decorations, etc. Gnarly has a season's greeting response.

"I use cat poop, lots of it, and the fresher the better because it will go further. You use a very sturdy cardboard box with a piece of wood in the bottom to cushion the large, coiled spring you will mount in the bottom of that box.

"Next, you fasten a piece of cardboard over the spring, like a launching platform. You put your bushel or so of fresh cat poop on this platform. Then you cover it with Saran wrap to hold in the odor. The final bit is to close the box, wrap it, and put it where some nasty mark will find it and rip it off."

Gnarly says it's always more fun if you can see this giant Poop-in-the-Box explode on the mark or marks. Otherwise, use your imagination.

"I got to see one explode once," Gnarly says, "and it was great. I never thought the stuff would fly so far. But that poop covered twenty feet, stuck to a ceiling that was twelve feet high, and the fallout ruined food and furniture over a thirty-foot arc. I had a hard time not laughing until I left the mark's place."

If you want to get even with your mark at night by attacking one of many mark's most cherished treasures, the car, follow Prankster's advice. He suggests you take a great, solid dump on a heavy, dark-colored towel just after you've gotten into your mark's car and removed the overhead lightbulb. Place the dump-laden towel on the driver's side seat or drape it over the gas pedal, depending upon the degree of nasty you feel toward this mark.

POPPERS

Old Grizzled is a fine chap, easygoing, but when you do something bad to him, you'll end up wishing the Pope had anathematized you rather than have Grizzled put you up in his fire and smoke.

For instance, a friend of Grizzled's has a neighbor with a very nasty goat that chases the friend's kids, messes up the friend's yard, and is otherwise not nice. Grizzled took care of this while the friend was on vacation.

"As it was just below freezing, I made up four of my special Poppers, a plastic Pepsi bottle in which I put a bunch of carbide I had stashed in those digestible horsepill capsules. Since the Pepsi was frozen, nothing happened right away.

"I planted my delayed-action Poppers in the goat's pen. We had a good January thaw that week and when the liquid ate away the capsule and set off that carbide, the mark thought someone was shooting at or bombing his goat," Grizzled explained with his whooping laugh.

The mark was furious in frustration, steaming about like a fresh cow pie in a snowbank. And there was nobody around.

Later, Grizzled secreted a couple of firewood bangers in the mark's woodpile, using rifle primers rather than live ammunition. I suggested that the next attack on the firewood be made with a live round from which the bullet has been pulled and the end of the casing sealed. Or use an M-80 for all I care.

PORNOGRAPHY

Because the forces of censorship, ignorance, fear, and bullyhood all seem to have an intense, almost pathological, obsession with pornography, this literature form is easy and convenient for making trouble for your mark. Given that well-known social phenomenon, the Swaggart-Baker Syndrome, it is often the most pious antiporn personalities who are the most kinky and sexually perverted among us. This makes Col. No Man's Fallout Exercise work even better. Here's how it works.

1. Using cash or a money order in your mark's name, order some kiddie porn for him or her. Do this several times. Each time ask the smut dealer to keep "your" name on his mailing files for "special promotions" of real kiddie porn.

2. If all goes according to plan, the mark will throw out the kiddie porn when it arrives. More importantly, if you tip someone off, that someone could then find it in his trash and cause it to get into the wrong hands.

3. Most local police are not sophisticated and tend to be very emotional about issues such as those raised in this stunt. Any rudimentary investigation will turn up the mark's established m.o., his past record of buying kiddie porn, etc. I am sure that angry parents, betrayed fellow censors, and outraged politicians will do the rest for you.

Don't feel sorry for your mark! He or she had to have done something dastardly to bring down this plague upon his or her house.

Don't fret for the rights of the porn seller, that merchant of venus mons, either. The profitable hairy pie of pornography is major big business requiring flaccid investment and raising engorged profits.

PUBLIC RELATIONS

Public relations is one of our major growth industries, whose product is often guile and façade where imagery replaces reality. But let's not get too snooty, because all of us are PR practioners at some time. Come on, even you refrain from belching, farting, and scratching your ass on at least the first couple of dates.

A major branch of professional public relations is publicity, getting you, your company, or your client's good image into the news media. It's all a matter of putting your best feat forward, I guess. Anyway, one day while sucking down a few cold lemonades with some friends, I heard a very funny story from Vaslo Phlegm about how he got revenge on a PR man who had really done some very unethical things.

"This publicity guy was a devious swine, given to lying, taking credit for other people's ideas, and using company funds, equipment, and time for personal projects," Vaslo told us. "Knowing that reporters and editors didn't really like the guy anyway, I decided to make that feeling even stronger."

As a premise, folks, you have to understand that most honest, tough, and intelligent journalists, which is about 40 percent of the entire profession, are really independent, stubborn people who view publicity people realistically, i.e., as humanoid garden slugs who want to suck up free space and time in the media. Most successful PR types are toady assbussers who are viewed by those 40 percent of media types who are real journalists with suspicious disdain. Therein lies the sting of Vaslo's plan.

"Pretending to be this PR dork, I called the assistants to department editors at the various regional media offices. I really laid into them, telling these journalists they did a rotten job of covering my company, that they couldn't write, that they were incompent jerks who were stuck in low-paying news jobs while winners like me were important PR types.

"I called assistants because I figured the editors would know this jerk personally while the others didn't. I was right and the message got passed along quickly. Some called the jerk back and really unloaded. The really urinated-off journalists didn't bother to call back. Instead, they figured other ways to get back at this fool. Good journalists are usually creative-thinking people, so you figure it out."

I told Vaslo I really liked his idea. How about you?

RADIO STATIONS

Speaking of radio talk shows, two of the funniest and friendliest hosts going are Jay Thomas at KPWR in Los Angeles and Jack Wheeler at WPLP, Tampa/St. Petersburg. Then, of course, there is my old favorite home, KFYI in Phoenix. That's because of all the grand friends in and near that city of sun.

RESTAURANTS

Houdini used to eat at a restaurant in his town. The owner used to come over to visit and sit with Houdini. The man was obese, smelled, and would order coffee or a sandwich, then stick it on Houdini's bill. Houdini says he tried many subtle ways to get the cheap lardass to stay away from his table. No luck.

"Finally, I decided if he was going to stick around I'd help him," Houdini says. "The next time he came over, I had friends with me and we had a table full of dishes and glasses. Old Lardass came over, sat down, and started being obnoxious.

"While his attention was on one of the girls at the table, I carefully and firmly used a large safety pin to attach his jacket to the tablecloth."

At this point, Houdini and his friends left. Three seconds later they heard a loud, continuous *craaaaasshhhh* as dishes and glasses smashed to the floor. Lardass had stood up.

"You didn't even have to turn around to imagine the picture and enjoy the scene," Houdini concluded.

ROADKILL

When Roy Blount, Jr., wrote his delightful C & W song, "I'm Just a Bug On the Windshield of Life," he didn't even know that Uncle Chris and Uncle David had eaten roadkill yet. In their usual tasteless way, Uncle Chris and Uncle David have come up with another use for these handy highway helpers for Haydukery.

Roadkill is wonderful for creating scary and intimidating pictures to send to your mark as postal cards or in a fancy frame. Or slip the pictures into frames of existing pictures in the homes and offices of the mark, his friends, and family. You may also put these pictures in the frames being sold in stores.

"You get a large, whole roadkill, like a groundhog, that's not been all smashed," Uncle Chris explains. "Lay it on its back and extend one paw. Between the toes of this paw you place an enlarged picture of your mark, preferably a formal portrait.

"You then step back and using either a close-up or macro-zoom lens on your camera, take some color photos of this setup, the dead animal holding a photo of your mark. Then send the developed and printed final photos as we suggested."

Uncle David and Uncle Chris also added that you could get very weird and kinky in your selection of mark photos, including composite photos. You can also make really different choices as to roadkill animal selection and where, specifically, the mark's photo will be placed for the setup picture. They thought you'd understand.

You've heard the expression about cooking one's goose? A friend of Dick Smegma literally cooked his landlord's cat. When he was losing his $400 security deposit to his crooked landlord through no fault of his own, Dick's pal was so mad that he didn't see the landlord's cat sleeping under his car tire when he left the driveway.

Obviously, the heavy truck tire flattened the feline. Not wishing to waste the moment, or too many tears, Dick's buddy took the cat with him, cooking up the idea of creating kitty quiche for the landlord.

Dick takes up the story, saying, "My friend was due to leave the apartment the next day and had already moved his stuff out. He was still furious. He took that cat corpse and put it in the apartment's built-in oven and left it to slow cook at 275 degrees for the next two days.

"Can you imagine what that larcenous landlord found when he came in for building inspection? The kitty's collar was draped over the oven door handle. It must have smelled wonderful in there.

"My friend had moved clear across the country and was easily out of the landlord's legal reach. He denied everything anyway, then just turned it all over to his brother, an attorney, to hassle the crooked landlord even more. A former neighbor there later wrote to my friend and said that his former place wasn't rented for two months because of the odor and the story about the whole situation. It was the talk of the whole apartment complex.

In one of my earlier books, I made a plea for photographs of any particularly gory roadkill you might happen upon while out on a Sunday drive. Well keep 'em coming—if I receive enough submissions, we might be able to put a special book together. Send your pics to me at the address on page 185. Thank you.

ROOSTERS

Who can forget Carla Savage? Surely nobody who's gone against this classy lady will soon forget. Now I learn her mother, Marty, is also adept at blasting away the bastards who make life uncivilized for others of us.

Marty had a neo-Nazi neighbor who complained about pet noise and any sort of fun behavior coming from the Savage side of the fence. Savage side. I like that. Anyway, this crypto-cretin called the police, shot BB guns at the dogs, and was a royal bastard. That's when Marty said she'd had enough of the chickenshit.

She got several roosters—loud, obnoxious, mean-tempered roosters—and dumped them into Mr. Nazi's yard at night. They crowed and otherwise made nasty noises. Mr. Nazi was away. Mrs. Nazi called him and raised hell about "his" roosters in their yard. She insisted he come home right away and take care of this.

"His stupid wife used to tell my mom everything," Carla told me. "Anyhow, the guy comes home and can't figure it out. Meanwhile, my mom tells him really sweetly that this rooster noise is very bad for the neighborhood and mentions calling the police."

He got rid of them. Marty got more. Mr. Nazi shot one of them that night when it crowed. Mom jumped over the fence and dumped its body in the guy's swimming pool. His wife raised hell about him wounding that poor bird such that it crash-landed into the pool and drowned.

Carla says that Mr. Nazi never did figure out what was

happening to him via the roosters. It just proves that old adage credited to Freddie Sykes, that sometimes it takes a noisy little cock to shut up a great big prick.

SALESPERSONS

A good salesperson is the high priest in the temple of business. Yet sometimes the sermon can get annoying, expensive, and irritating. To put the salesperson in perspective, it is sometimes necessary to put mind over patter. Which reminds me of a story The Ranger told me.

A friend of his had a very obnoxious car salesman as his next-door neighbor. We'll call him Howard. Howard was a bully, a gossip, and a drunk. He also screwed his neighbors on car deals, and, in two cases, literally, their wives.

As Howard was a car salesman he had a Demonstrator, his own car from work, a dealer sample, as it were. The Ranger's friend found Howard's Demo and poured a pint of warm milk under the front seat and another pint of warm milk in the trunk.

After a week of unhappiness, Howard had to have major replacements for the Demo's interior, at his own expense, of course.

Seedy had quite another experience. Fresh from college, he was a new salesman with ambition, goals, and fresh outlooks. Unhappily, he worked with a jerk who was foreman of the shipping department, a very sensitive job to a salesperson's life. The older man was highly jealous of Seedy and had already driven other salespeople from the company. Management seemed blind to the problem.

Seedy said he had to get the man's attention to change his perception of salespeople. He also had to get either fear or respect from this man. He set him up with the cooperation of the guys who worked on the loading dock, all of whom hated the foreman.

"Some of us ate lunch outside on nice sunny days at a small picnic area the plant had. We pulled the stunt on the mark-foreman there. I made sure that I sat next to the foreman, then one of the guys diverted his attention. I quickly daubed some peanut butter on the edge of my shoe and waited for the foreman to turn back," Seedy said.

At this point, one of the other guys piped up, "Hey, Seedy, is that dog shit on your shoe?" Everyone agreed it was and laughed.

Seedy said, "Damned if I didn't step in dog shit somewhere. I wonder how fresh it is?"

With that, Seedy put his finger down and plucked the peanut butter off his shoe and popped it into his mouth with gusto, making a big sound and look of satisfactory delight. He yummed and awwed about how good fresh dog shit tasted.

True story: The foreman looked, gulped, gagged, and vomited his lunch and breakfast all over himself. He took the rest of the day off.

"From that moment on he was always nice to me," Seedy added. "I became especially nice to him, asking him how he felt when he reported back to work and all of that. It was nearly a week until he'd eat with us again. But I never had any more problems with him."

SCHOOLS

Why is it that so many school administrators are such mental midgets? I once had the misfortune to sit in a class full of educational administrators for three days. Not being one of them, I fled. Actually, it was almost worse than being captured by the bad guys in wartime, which also happened to me...but I digress.

John Elliott McGeary made a hobby of fighting back against bigots, bastards, bullies, and other evildoers in high school at Vandergrift, Pennsylvania. In one case he shot a duck and snuck it into an empty locker the next day, incarcerating it with a heavy padlock. A decaying duck smells much worse than you might imagine...far worse than a chicken, crow, or other bird with less body fat. After six days of suffering, the school was closed an additional three days while "readjustment and repair" was accomplished.

Other accomplishments credited to John McGeary include the following:

• After catching a number of suckers and catfish from the nearby river, he put them in a large metal drum into which he urinated six or seven times daily. Within two weeks he had a horrible brew cooking, so bad that he had to approach it with an air mask filter. He filled a plastic mustard squeeze bottle with the ugly juice from this brew, took it to school, and sprayed it on the handrails of several staircases. The memory, the stench, and the heartbreak of people's hand infections lingered for days.

• Assisted by his pal Burl Yates, John experimented with

130

oxygen-filled balloons. They found that by mixing acetylene with oxygen, they could create a highly explosive toy. Experimenting with various fuses, lengths of string, etc., the bombastic boys learned how to explode the balloons as they reached the ceilings of the auditorium, or, when released outside, when they reached the second-story classroom windows.

I was told that John Elliott McGeary is either doing time in Vacaville Prison in California, passed away in Markle, Pennsylvania, or is an assistant to Larry Flynt.

While he was attending school, my pal Pepper also worked as an assistant janitor for the money and the potential for infamy. He realized this potential quickly when one of the snooty bitches dunked his kid sister's gym suit in a toilet for no special reason other than that she wasn't an "in" kid.

Pepper says he waited, saying and doing nothing. Then, as he was cleaning up the bio labs after dissection class, he began to collect some of the grosser specimens and parts thereof.

"I did the usual, like flayed worm bookmarks in the bitch's books and rat entrails in her boots, but my happiest was a whole fetal pig in her lunch box. She was out of school for a week," Pepper recalls.

He adds the amusing part that another assistant janitor, a nasty, shiftless toadstool of a student, caught the blame as he had been pestering the bitch for a date. Pepper says, "That was the day I learned the meaning of the word serendipity."

Dr. Clint Taurus hated noisy students when he was trying to study as a serious graduate student. "Fun is neat," he says, "but there is a time for study and we were blessed by an entire floor of asinine, overgrown, underbrained football players living below us."

The Doctor was on Floor Three, the Animals on Floor Two. He complained to their zookeeper, an assistant coach, who laughed at him. The Doctor thought he would rain on their continual party.

"These assholes partied all of the time because the school just had them there to play ball, not to be real students. They stayed up all night and kept us awake, too. So a few times I watched them party on a large balcony just below a hall window on our floor."

The Doctor pissed out of that window several times, hitting the various beer pitchers below and partially refilling them. Yet this had no effect. So, being in the National Guard, he had boots to be shined.

"I had a really filthy rag I buffed them with. It was all brown and black. I started using an old pair of underwear I had swiped from the assistant coach/zookeeper downstairs. He had his name sewn in the shorts."

After two weeks the underwear looked just like the guy had blown mud in his drawers. Dr. Taurus went to his window and played bombadier, hitting the pitcher perfectly. After his "bomb" splashed into the pitcher, he soon heard the loud, drunken louts screaming, cursing the unwitting coach, and even a few vomiting.

"I slept well that evening and for several others. There was a major send-up about the entire incident, but the assistant coach caught the shit, appropriately enough."

SEPTIC TANKS

A lot of marks live in the country these days, including the suburban country where they still use septic tanks because city sewer systems haven't come that way yet. There are many things you can do to a mark's septic system that will cause nasty, smelly things to happen.

Grizzled relates an old farm trick from his childhood when kids used to fill the mean, nasty neighbor's outhouse pit with lots of yeast. He says the same principle works with today's modern home septic tank system.

"You can get to the mark's septic tank in most cases through the cleanout access, usually a two-foot round cement or tile pipe that leads above ground from the tank itself," Grizzled explains. "You lift off that lid and dump copious amounts of dry yeast down there. I'm talking several pounds. Close the lid and leave."

Now you know the value of that chemistry class in school. Right...the pressure builds as the yeast works and the odoriferous gases begin to back up through the various water traps meant to stop same from happening. When the pressure is strong enough, those wonderful gases full of foul odor will pump right back into the mark's home, making it smell just like...? You got it.

SHORTS

Despite becoming a parody of himself, Johnny Carson has said some funny things. One of the funniest to me is his use of the word "shorts" when discussing men's underwear. I can't explain it but I find that word hilarious in his generational, midwestern context. Or maybe I just imagine Big Ed lumbering around guffawing at his master's voice while dressed in huge, billowy, nearly knee length white shorts, socks, and garters. Oh well...

Ex-big leaguer Jay Johnstone also mentions shorts in his funny book. As a practical joke, he once smeared Capsolin in a fellow player's shorts. For those of you who never played sports, Capsolin is the hottest of the hot stuff that comes out of a tube. It is today's high tech version of the fifties analgesic balm in the jockstrap.

One tip. Capsolin is red. You have to disguise it with some color-masking powder or make sure your mark has red shorts or whatever it is you're loading with this Major League heat.

I realize my token liberal reader will worry about the possibility of this substance burning the mark's genitals. My answer is a simple and humble: Who the hell cares!

SKI WAX

Not being a skier, I take Capt. Video's word for this, since he managed it against a nasty villain personally. The wax that skiers use on their skis is very slick, obviously. The Captain had to deal with a nasty prick of a supervisor and after trying to be civilized, he turned to the ski wax for relief.

"I had access to his boots in the winter and waxed the soles very thoroughly. He put on those boots and stepped out the door onto a patch of ice. *Whoooossshhhhh!*! The fat jerk almost broke a record for distance and impact," said the Captain joyfully.

Even better, the jerk got up and tried to walk four more times before he figured out it was something more than ice that was causing the painful, embarrassing problem.

"It didn't change his attitude or disposition, and the knowledge that someone was after him didn't civilize him at all. But it didn't detract from my feeling good about his slippery misfortune or the other things I had done to this prick."

SMOKE

Eating and drinking with friends can be bad for you. Sometimes the food and booze are so wretched that your urine will burn holes right through your kidneys. But don't turn down invites to cookouts on my warning. Remember what our friend Smokey the Bare said about trouble: Where there's smoke, there might be one of those liquid smoke products, that stuff you use when you cook burgers and steaks inside but want them to smell and taste like outside.

Smokey says to dump the stuff on your mark's car, furniture, office, files, clothes, etc. The uses for this product, universally available in all supermarkets, is endless. From personal experience I know that it really does, ahhh, have a very strong odor.

Nonetheless, there's nothing stronger or more obnoxious than the odor of cigarette smoke. But you already know how I feel about smokers' intrusions into my air and life. Houdini feels the same way and has devised a fun scheme to burn people who insist on using their ciggie smoke to make his life miserable.

"I break the red tips off some matches, usually a half dozen or so, and insert them into the mark's cigarette or cigar. What will happen is obvious and very amusing," Houdini says.

Houdini says his pal Eddie believes that the meek will inherit the earth, but only after everyone else is done with it.

SMOKERS

When he gave up smoking, I applauded LTC Mac. He realized that giving up this vice would allow him more time and energy for his others. In any case, I was visiting him not long ago at a secret camp in Central America, near the small village of La Penga. As we walked into his small quarters, many of his officers were smoking away, a time-honored military tradition. My involuntary cough control center cut loose, sounding as if I'd just chugged a mug of Tic Tac. Phew...

One of his bronzed warriors sneered at me and snapped, "If my smoking bothers you, leave the gawdamn area!"

The rest of the brass chortled at the snappy put-down delivered to the arrogant civilian, me. LTC Mac smiled his gas-pain smirk at me and said, "I apologize for my officers. You must know that some are too old to remember their manners, while some are too young to have any."

We laughed while he explained my work to them, how I was an area rep for the Motilones and their Motilón Company from Venezuela.

Chris Schaefer is a bit more direct in his dealing with smokers. He likes to light up their lives in an educational fashion. When Chris is bothered by rude people who smoke in no smoking areas or who blow smoke on other people, he pulls out his small artillery.

"I have a tiny squirt gun filled with lighter fluid. When a smoker escalates his activity beyond rude and gets aggressive about it, I just pull out my squirt gun and zap the guy's smoke. *Poof!!!"*

Chris says this stunt is most effective in crowded, noisy areas where the mark is not likely to catch where the blast came from.

Madman Mike has his own menu for dealing with obnoxious people who actively intrude their smoke upon our lives. Some of his safer suggestions follow:

• Put several pinholes into unsmoked cigarettes.

• Bury several match heads deep into a cigarette. The smoking mark will have miniature Roman candle in his or her mouth.

• Fingernail clippings will do the same thing as horse hair when hidden in a cigarette, i.e., make it stink worse than normal.

• Need to booby trap an unopened pack? Mike says to use a pin to peel the pack open from the bottom. Do it neatly and carefully. Sabotage the ciggies, rewrap the pack, and use a tiny dot of clear model cement to seal the cellophane.

SNOT

Mention snot to most folks and they ugly up their faces as if they'd just kissed the wrong end of a freshly wet baby. That's sad, because as I've pointed out before, snot is so very appropriate for making a grand statement. Versatile, it goes well with food, clothing, personal products, dental equipment, visual aids, etc.

Jerry Jeff Walker, that reknowned singer and substance receptacle, is a man whose fun and music I admire a lot. The man who wrote "Mr. Bojangles," Brother Walker has had an amazingly interesting life. He is also a Master Snot Spreader.

During an interview, Walker once said, "Yeah, I have a lot of mucus up there, and I sometimes use it to decorate the offices and homes of folks I'm pissed with." Friends and other witnesses told me they'd seen him blow it hard five or six feet straight on the wall of a major record company's New York executive offices, in the private office of a major Hollywood producer, and in the pastel living room of a fussy major celebrity.

Isn't that great!

As long as you give credit, it isn't wrong to steal Jerry Jeff Walker's mannerism and skill of being able to force-fully blow snot all over anyone and anything that deserves to be your mucus-laden mark.

SOURCES

I get very few letters of complaint. Those that do come in complain most about companies listed in this Sources section either not responding to calls or mail, having moved without leaving forwarding information. When I list these companies, all I can assure you is that they were in business when I wrote this section, usually two or three months before the book comes out. I really have no control over what any of these people do or don't do. If I've dealt with them personally I will note that in the text. Otherwise, you're on your own. I offer these solely as a helpful service.

However, as Capt. Video also points out, be careful with whom you deal by mail or telephone. Some mail drops, for instance, require you to complete a postal service form before they'll handle your business. The next to last thing you want in a mail drop is a trail of autographed paper the feds can trace back to you. Overall, just use common sense, honest dealing, and care, lots of care.

American Fireworks News, Star Route, Box 30, Dingman's Ferry, PA 18328. (717) 828-8417.

A lot of you would enjoy an interesting publication from this publisher. It's the *Fireworks Buyers Guide and Trade Directory*, an annual compilation of fireworks wholesalers and retailers, plus component product suppliers and dealers. A lot of how-to-buy info is found within these pages.

Aztec International, 1256 E. Oakbrook Dr., Norcross, GA 30093. (404) 446-2304.

These folks sell the real nasty stuff for top-of-the-line, serious Haydukers. We're talking fuse, booby trap components, alarms, gas grenades, igniters, signal cartridges, flares—the entire arsenal.

Comb, 1405 Xenium Lane, Plymouth, MN 55441. 1-800-328-0629.

A liquidation center, this mail-order outfit has top-quality products at amazingly low prices. Everything from tools through electronics. I buy there; it's a great place.

E.J. Dailey's Lures & Baits, P.O. Box 38, Union Hill, NJ 14563.

Brother Dailey sells potions to attract animals genetically beyond cute 'n fuzzy, i.e., heavy duty critters like raccoons, coyotes, lions, bears, et. al. Between your plans and Dailey's products, your mark's yard, office, or whatever will become a very wild zoo.

Executive Protection Products, 1834 First St., Suite 1, Napa, CA 94559. (707) 253-7142.

These guys sell some pretty big league stuff, e.g., gas grenades, smoke grenades, real bugs and antibugs, taps and tap traps, laser sights, and other paranoid goodies.

Jerryco, 601 Linden Place, Evanston, IL 60202. (312) 475-8440.

This is one of the oddest really neat catalogs I have. It's like having access to a science lab at a major university and a well-stocked hardware store. There are great gadgets and components for Haydukery, as well as a lot of just plain neat stuff. They have retail outlets in Chicago and Milwaukee.

Johnson Smith Co., 4514 19th Court E., Bradenton, FL 34203. (813) 747-9754.

Anyone over the age of forty remembers these guys—

great pranks, tricks, and class-clown paraphernalia for us, and the bane of our parents. JS is back, moved from Detroit to Florida, and has the same silly, insane stuff for practical jokers and, of course, Haydukers. Yes, I still buy from them.

Loompanics Unlimited, P.O. Box 1197, Port Townsend, WA 98368.

Mike Hoy runs a really different business here. He sells some of the most unusual and controversial books in the free world. His best endorsement is that advertising for some of his books is banned by such bastions of acceptable taste as *Soldier of Fortune* magazine. Their catalog is one of the best.

Paladin Press, P.O. Box 1307, Boulder, CO 80306.

Paladin's the top publisher for the kind of book you need to plan the perfect revenge. Publisher of the Hayduke library of masterpieces, Paladin shows you how to protect your right to live, and how to make or get the tools to do it right.

Pranks Inc., P.O. Box 11632, Salt Lake City, UT 84147

From the land of not-too-funny Mormontown comes a neat idea. It's a floppy disk full of useful computer-generated practical jokes, insults, etc. to turn your mark's PC into an electronic booby trap. Some are funny, many are nasty. I've used *Pranks* myself and award it my highest Good Hayduking Seal of Approval.

Shomer-Tec, P.O. Box 2187, Bellingham, WA 98227. (206) 733-6214.

Formerly Alcan Distributors, these people offer a magnificent selection of military and law enforcement supplies and equipment. Their materiel is professional quality, too. This is not knock-off crapola for the civilian market. Their catalog is most useful. I have dealt with these folks and they're pro, all the way.

Square Lake Enterprises, P.O. Box 3673, Logan, UT 84321.

These folks specialize in special effects, offering fast, free shipping on all sorts of technical grade chemicals, rocket supplies, electrical igniters, time fuses, tools, and supplies. They have a catalog.

Universal Electronics, 15015 Ventura Blvd., Sherman Oaks, CA 91403. (818) 906-7789.

This place is the K-Mart of high-tech tools, weapons, combat equipment, electronic surveillance gear, explosives, and dozens of books telling you just how to use all of these goodies and much, much more. This is the kind of book your good parents would never let you keep when you were a chronological kid.

STEREO

Noise is where it finds you, which is often when and where you don't want it to be. I refer to the nasty neighbor with the loud stereo that keeps you awake or distracted at the wrong time, usually when you don't want to play Haydn seek, or have someone's noise rock your roll.

The Razor will help you cut out that source of irritation. He tells me that musicians used to purposely poke small holes in their amp speakers to get really good sound distortion in the days before such effects became technological options. This bit of musical history knowledge is power for you.

"Use a sharp razor knife, ice pick, or paper clip to poke small holes in your mark's speaker system. Obviously you have to remove the outer grill to do this.

"Once in there, just poke two holes in the woofer and one in the tweeter. Replace the grill. Wait to hear the results of your modification," Razor says.

Unless the mark is a hearing-blasted heavy metal freak, he or she will know shortly that the system is ruined. With luck, they might blame their own loud use of the system. With luck.

Actually, any sort of sound system which uses a speaker can be hit with this stunt. Consider radios, telephones, cassette players, headphones, ghetto blasters, hearing aids, etc. In any case, Handel with care.

STORES

Ray Heffer says he should have known better when he tried to shop at the furniture store in that famous city. The salesclerk got so excited about Ray coming into the store that he actually looked up from the paperwork he was reading, looked at Ray, yawned, and nodded. The rest of the visit went downhill from there.

"Basically, they sold me used merchandise as new, then refused to give me my money back when I complained," Ray said. "The manager said I had damaged the sofa and that it had been new when I got it. Not so, I told him. He told me to sue them."

Instead, Ray remembered a friendly neighborhood druggist from his childhood, an old chap who'd told him all about Nux Vomica, a chemical compound in powder form that can be used to induce vomiting.

"It smells awful and leaves a strong odor where it lands," Ray explained. "The idea is to go back into that store and have a distraction created so you can sprinkle some of that powder on the couches and other furniture on display.

"It will stink very much and has to be professionally cleaned. Be careful not to inhale fumes or any of the powder because it will make you physically ill," Ray adds.

In thinking over Ray's last warning there, I think I could come up with some other uses for Nux Vomica that would be appropriate for the Additives or Chemical sections of this book.

The Prankster got really urinated-off at a store because

the owner fired his friend for suspicion of stealing money from the store. Truth was, it was the owner's son who was the thief. Worse, the owner bad-mouthed Prankster's pal. Prankster and his pal had a neat way of washing out the owner's mouth.

Prankster said, "I got into the store (nobody knew me from any other customer) and went to the soda cooler. I got two cans of soda out, opened the pop-tops just enough to drain them, and did so. I used a hypodermic to refill each can with soapy detergent water mixed with urine, pushed the tab back and resealed it all with less than a drop of Super Glue. Then I put the cans back in the cooler."

Another of Prankster's paybacks for this owner was to borrow the store brooms and snow shovels, sneak them away for a brief time, and saw through half of the handle near the base or bottom. He then filled the saw line with coloring.

"That way, when the mark or his clerk goes to sweep or shovel, the handle will snap off," says Prankster. "Do all of his handled equipment while you're at it."

SUCCESS STORY

As Branch Rickey used to say, "Luck is the residue of success." That's why I am always happy to receive reader mail with clips about successful Hayduking stunts from around the world.

This story was sent to me by Leann Melanzana and is a clip from the *China Daily News* from Beijing, August 1987. It tells of a Beijing restaurant owner who got even with three teenage boys who hassled his customers and molested his daughter by killing the lads, cooking some of their body parts, then serving them to the unknowing parents when they came in his establishment.

After three days, the parents reported the missing boys to the police. After investigation, followed by a neighbor's complaint of awful odors coming from the restaurant kitchen, police found the remains of the boys in the walk-in freezer. The man got a life sentence.

SUPERMARKETS

His name is Dr. Zombie and he is a First Time Hayduker. His story is that he was hired by the local branch of a large supermarket chain for a summer job. Normally, Dr. Zombie is a nice young person who works hard, well, and honestly. This time, though, Dr. Zombie got a NO SALE when it came to merit raises at the payroll office.

"The manager gave what paltry raises there were to his daughter and three of her pals, plus one boyfriend. It sucked. Several of us worked a lot harder, but got nothing. One of my friends asked the boss about it and got laid off," Dr. Zombie said.

What followed was an elaborate and effective payback, the details of which follow.

"The checkout system involved scanner-type pricing units based on the Universal Price Code (UPC) system. A friend and I had been switched to night shift because we were identified as being with the complainers even though we'd said nothing about the pay raises.

"We invested in a couple of very inexpensive permanent color markers and began to black out the UPC bars on random selections of merchandise, doing large numbers of some items and fewer of others," Dr. Zombie reported.

Using that as a warm-up, they waited for any improvement in working conditions. When conditions grew worse and more suspicious instead, they began their magic marker warfare in earnest, increasing the numbers of items blacked-out.

"By one Sunday we had the store managers who had to work that day in a panic. There was chaos at the checkout counter. And nobody suspected us, a couple of stupid stock boys. I hope we taught that jerk a lesson, but I doubt it."

SWEETIES

A friend who feels minimally negative about his divorce from his paid-more, laid-more ex-wife once told me, "Alimony is like pumping gasoline into another guy's car." Or as King Francis I is supposed to have said, "Often does a woman change and very foolish is he who trusts her." I imagine you could have gotten the same reaction in gender reversal from some of the ladies around him.

My old pal, Ray Heffer, told me about being in Divorcetown, Nevada, and seeing all of the ex's lying around hotel pools, waiting like snakes to slough off the old husband or wife skins and seek new prey for mating purposes. Ray says he knew one especially obnoxious lady who carried her own vaginal jelly on dates. Ray wanted to do his part.

"I got some fine, bleached sand and her tube of jelly at the same time. I poked the sand down into the jelly with a wooden match, then put the top back on the tube. I probably don't need to mention any clinical details about the results."

Ray is a master of understatement.

Meanwhile, the Midnight Avenger got the shaft from his ex-girlfriend in a most uncivilized fashion and decided to get back after a sensible cooling period. In his school, locker inspections are both fashionable and predictable. As his ex-sweetie had become a semi-wild bird, his plan was easy.

"I was able to get to the file where they kept all of the combinations for the built-in locks on students' locker doors. I found my ex-lady's combination and got to her locker before school started on the day I knew an inspection was

150

scheduled," Mr. Avenger recalled.

His next step was to place some very explicit porn books in the locker with a faked inscription in each, something along the lines of "Wish we could act these out again soon," and signed by a teacher who had also unfairly done in Mr. Avenger. He also put a small amount of local weed in the locker.

"As usual she was late for homeroom and didn't get into her locker. The inspection came an hour later and she was called into the office. I smiled a lot. Her folks had to come in for a conference and that teacher was even more grim and hard-assed than usual for a couple of weeks. Me? I smiled a lot."

Millard Turd was dumped by his girlfriend because he couldn't afford to take her to the swanky bistros in their town. He told me this girl was a real bitch—very greedy, self-centered, and all the above.

"She was also a mommy and daddy's little girl type of woman. You know, she's twenty-seven, but acts ten when the folks are around. That was sickening, too. But I was able to use all of this," Millard reports.

Millard did a lot of business travel and had access to various telephones. He would place a collect call to the Little Princess, as he called her, and tell the operator that he was the girl's daddy. The old man was always on the road so this worked.

"She'd come on the line and ooohh and ahhh her way through five minutes of goo, then ask me how I was. I'd imitate her father's voice and start talking about all the gross and very sexually explicit stuff I'd like to do with her body.

"She'd be hysterical and start pleading for me to stop. Then she realized it wasn't her daddy and she really went to pieces. I kept at it until she hung up."

Millard did this several more times, then had a new girlfriend, who also had a very nasty mind, do the same basic stunt, claiming to be the girl's mother. It worked even better that way.

I have mentioned Pyridium before, but not with the devastating force that Carla Savage brings to the game. If some prick of a mark deserves it, this warm young lady can break his balls at one hundred yards without blinking one of her lovely eyes. She's tried this and it works well.

"I had one of those sweeties who thought it was fine for him to whore around while I had to wait at home all wrapped in protective double standard," Carla said quietly, reaching for her supply of red Pyridium.

"Carefully, I slipped some of this goody to my roaming sweetie, and golly, his urine turned this sickly reddish color. The best part is that he could see directly where it was coming from."

The kick is that most of these macho marks won't go to the Doc. They figure it will go away. So Carla dosed off for a week. Her mark/sweetie got the cocky roamings again. She dosed him again.

Carla says this happened three times before the jerk went to the medical folks. Carla said she was, at this point, hanging around only to enjoy the fun. By the time he went to the Doc's, she was tired of the game and split for good.

Carla's dosage: two tabs the first time out. Pyridium is not cheap and has a short shelf life. In most states you need a prescription, but in most instances that is easy to get. In Mexico you don't need a prescription.

As a postscript, Carla says, "If your gentleman attempts to inflict his 'diseased instrument' on you during his 'crisis,' that is proof that you've made the correct decision."

Speaking of macho jerks, as a working athlete, CD knows all kinds of that species. He reports a wonderful put-down delivered by a wonderful lady to a particularly obnoxious sports cretin. The drunken lout was boasting of his bedroom prowess in his usual English-as-second-language style when

152

she interrupted him.

"I've heard of you," she said in practiced awe. "You're the one with the jockstrap made from a peanut shell and rubber band."

Midwestern Will met a young lady once whose sole delight was tormenting other people. She would pit young men against each other in the most cruel and base fashion. She was mean and catty about other young women. She played friends off against each other. Does the word "bitch" come to mind? Will thought his fun would be to help her live up to her reputation where it counted most, at home with good old mom and dad.

Will's first step was to concoct a letter from a macho jockjerk at school and send it to the girl's mother. The letter basically apologized for "a moment of unthinking passion between two adolescents on five occasions...realization that daughter is with child." Will had the unsuspecting secondary mark, also a bully and a scoundrel, explain to mom that her daughter had wanted an abortion, but he, the father-to-be, wanted her to have the child. Would mom help him to convince daughter to have the child? We'll leave the outcome of this touching, real-life family drama to your imagination.

Isn't it amazing how valuable a silly little thing like sex can be to a dedicated and creative Hayduker? I mean, the fundamental components of sex are almost trivial: the proper mix of friction and lubrication, some personality and body temperature, all as trace elements. The main ingredient is probably a sense of the dramatic. Of course, there is the matter of packaging, marketing, and advertising.

SWIMMING POOLS

Just when you thought it was safe to dip into your pool,
The Klingon Bastard shows up to give your mark a hosing.
It worked like this. Mr. Bastard's pal lived next to a guy
with a swimming pool in his yard. This attractive nuisance
drew crowds of the neighbor's noisy and nasty friends who
partied all night and threw trash into our pal's pal's yard.

Turning all the various cheeks and trying to be a good
neighbor failed and the ultimate cheek-slap happened when
one portly poolside guest mooned the sleepless neighbor.
Outraged, our victim called on The Klingon Bastard.

"I advised my friend to take a small vacation and toward
the end of it I would make my move after studying the situation," Mr. Bastard told me. "The act itself was simple. I
drained the mark's pool, figuring it was the central actor that
was attracting all the noise and bad manners."

Mr. Bastard is being modest. It was how he did the job
that's fun. He created a simple siphon using a hose, water,
and a funnel. He brought the large funnel and hose with him.
The water came from the pool. Here's how it works.

Stick one end of the hose in the water. With the funnel
placed in the other end of the hose, hold it above the water
level of the pool. Dip some water from the pool and start
pouring it into the funnel, always keeping the funnel filled.

As you do this, keep your eye on the end of the hose
that's in the pool. Air bubbles should be coming out of it.
Keep pouring water into the funnel until the air bubbles stop
coming out the other end of the hose.

At this point you are ready to empty the pool. Mr. Bastard and I suggest removing the funnel from the hose and attaching that now-empty end of the hose to another piece of hose. The other end of that hose should already be inserted into the basement window of your mark's home. With hook-ups complete, you should soon have water gushing out the other end of that hose, creating an indoor pool for the mark.

Walk away.

TELEPHONE

We are slaves to this wonderful invention. It interrupts the most important moments of our live, like lovemaking, dinner, sitting on the can...

Consider. You've just sat down to a wonderful dinner and the phone explodes into your culinary happiness. You answer and some commercially happy voice tells you that you need to buy aluminum siding, or your roof needs to be redone, or there is a special on dictionaries that you can't pass up.

You can hang up, curse, scream...but they keep on calling. Here is what one man did to get back at his telephone tormentors.

"I found out who the CEO (aka the boss) of the solicitation company was and started to call him at inopportune times. I told him I was selling vertical burial vaults as life-after-death condos. I had my wife try to sell him custom-fitted condoms. Later, I called very late at night to sell him sleeping tablets.

"He finally blew his stack at me and screamed *why*? since I was obviously the same voice doing all the calls. I told him I was one of his company's involuntary customers and what more right did he have to invade my home privacy than I did his?"

Mr. Owner told our hero to come down to the office and have his name/number removed from their computer bank. It worked.

There is a commercial outfit also willing to help you.

There are many times when you want to hang up on a caller who is bothering or boring you. The list of specific callers in this category is endless. There is a product called "Hang Up Helper" which is a special paper that, when rubbed near a telephone receiver, sounds just like telephone line static. So when that talkative bore calls and you want off the line, just rub a little Hang Up Helper near your phone mouthpiece and announce that you can't hear a word your caller is saying. Then rub the paper louder. Scream in a very faint voice, "I'll try to call you back" and increase the static sound. Hang up.

As of this writing, this neat stuff is available from Hang Up Helper, P.O. Box 5474, Austin, TX 78763.

The French playwright Ferenc Molnar solved the problem of really unwelcome callers with whom he never wanted to speak by instructing his secretary to tell them, "I'm so sorry, he's not in. But he just left a moment ago, so if you rush down the street you'll probably catch up with him."

Our pal The Midnight Avenger has the number of those nasty unlisted telephones, too. Is your mark tormenting you from his highly mobile phone? The Avenger says to have someone who sounds official call the mark and pose as a telephone company official, obviously using a pay phone (so the call can't be traced), and ask for the mark's private code number for the mobile, cordless phone.

When you get that number I am sure you can think of all sorts of uses, including the 900-series numbers, many of which contain explicit messages. Ahhh, ain't technology grand!

Lots of people have shared this next idea with me. Your telephone number at home is similar to the number of a business, industry, or whatever. You get a lot of their calls. Do what Ruddy Fart, Mr. Avenger, and Blam Blam did — simply answer the calls and be nice.

Ruddy Fart explains, "All of us gets these calls asking about hours, specials, and stuff like that because our number is similar to that of the store. After begging the nearby 7-Eleven to change their number and being rudely told to 'fornicate off,' I decided to have some fun.

"Every time anyone called me for the 7-Eleven number, I went along with anything they asked for or made it better. I offered all kinds of deals and discounts. Finally, their attorney called me and I told him to 'fornicate off and leave me alone.'"

Three days later, the 7-Eleven management changed their local store's telephone number.

But the all-time nasty was related to me by Dick Smegma (who else?). He told me about a guy who got a royal sodomizing on installation and service charges by his local telephone company. He spent a lot of time, effort, and legal money to win his argument. However, the telephone company was able to hire more expensive lawyers who knew more expensive judges, same country club set and all that, so they won. The honest guy lost in court.

Enter aviation to the sense of restored justice. A friend of this man owned a Cessna aircraft. Together, they devised a steel cable and hook which they fastened to the aircraft, stowing the cable and hook inside the aircraft until airborne and ready to attack.

"They swooped down on rural, single-strand telephone lines owned by this company, using the cable and hook to rip the wires off the poles. The two men and their merry flying machine ripped out thirty telephone lines on their afternoon mission," Dick told me.

Effective. Thousands of customers complained, lots of overtime was paid, and the PUC got on the phone company's case. The FAA investigated and found nothing. This is not a new stunt. The late LTC Phillip Cochran told me that his fighter pilots did the same thing to Japanese military telephone and power lines in Burma during World War II.

Squeamish also delights in having fun with telephone

solicitors who won't take negative responses. He says he talks to them for a while and asks some questions, making his voice a bit more excited each time he asks something.

"I then heave off a heavy moan and scream into the phone, 'I'm cumming, ohhhh, I'm cumming,' and groan again. Then I clear my throat and say in my normal voice, 'Oh, thank you so very much, that was delightful and felt so good. Thank you.'"

Squeamish says this upsets solicitors of the same sex much more than the opposite gender. I dunno, I thought it was pretty funny.

A serious user of pay telephones, Discordia Dea agrees that these useful instruments should never be trashed. However, that doesn't mean you can't stick it to Ma Bell for the coins involved. Dea suggests that you simply epoxy the locks on the coin boxes, which does no damage to the instrument or its function. Super glue or liquid solder will do the trick.

Rapid Revenge used to have a live-in who ran up his phone bills and refused to pay her share. He got back at her by calling her collect from other cities where he traveled, but telling the operator he was her father or one of her brothers. The markess would gas away for five minutes or so while Rapid would mutter a few "uhhuh's" to keep her monologue on the line.

"My best record was fifteen minutes for her yakking on one call. This always worked because her family traveled a lot. I can imagine some of the scenes when her dad or brothers got home and faced this ditzy broad about some bizarre collect call they'd never made," Rapid reported.

Ray Heffer offers wonderfulness if your mark is an apartment person. He says, "You know how thin walls between rooms are and how tightly packed people are in modern apartments.

"You pick a weekend or evening when your mark is going

to be away. Go to a pay phone and call the mark's home. Obviously, you will hear the ringing signal. Lay the phone down...*don't hang it up*...and leave," says Ray.

The deal is that the phone will continue to ring and ring and ring and ring because nobody is there to answer it and because you left the line open by laying down a ringing phone. The reward is that so many neighbors will be highly urinated-off and complain enough that your mark might be forced to move.

You surely recall V.P. Kowalski and his stunt of using suntan creme on the earpiece of a telephone. He's back because he feels that he and I shorted the other end of the communication cycle, the mouthpiece.

"I want to correct that oversight, George," Kowalski recently told me. "So let's coat the mark's telephone mouthpiece with something disgusting."

Some of the mouthpiece coatings that came to Kowalski's mind included phlegm, pus, snot, ass-wipe, and wound-drip. I won't list the gross items, however. Kowalski also suggested unscrewing the mouthpiece and filling the cavity with animal feces, ants, ticks, fleas, or the like.

TELEVISION SETS

For a quiet guy from Missouri, Ray Heffer has a wonderful imagination, and I thank him very much for all the helpful ideas he has shared with us over the years. One of Ray's latest involves TV sets. Ever humane, Ray warns that you should be very carefully selective with this one, as injuries could occur. That, of course, has my attention already.

As always, Ray's right on target when he says a lot of marks would be better off minus their TV sets. He has a plan to help achieve that wonderful goal. Using a glass cutter and access to your mark's TV set, make a very pronounced cut into the face of the tube. Do it on the outer perimeter of the tube where it won't be so obvious.

Ray says to be sure you cut the tube glass and not any sort of covering glass. Check this carefully. What happens next is that the vacuum in the tube will draw on the cut and eventually implode the tube. Glass will fly. Your mark will be unhappy. Ray and I are laughing already.

On the gentler side of humor, Tyra Pierce is back again to share his latest conquest of inconsiderate and bullying roommates. His idea will work well with any mark whose TV needs to be sabotaged for whatever payback you owe.

Tyra had roomies and guests who came into his place, used his cable TV, and stayed and stayed and stayed. He got little rest, no studying, and was paying for the televised entertainment for these drunken louts who were apparently too stupid even to qualify for a fraternity membership.

Tyra solved the problem by scrambling his TV picture.

He did this by wrapping a tiny piece of aluminum foil around the male wire that was inserted into the female connector on the cable outlet. He left for a few days to visit a friend.

"The roomies and guests got so upset they made me call a repairman and promised to pay him. I did it. I also undid my foil scrambler before he arrived. He got there and the set worked fine. They paid him $25 for doing nothing more than turning on the TV set. They were very upset," Tyra said.

After the repairman left and his roomies went out to get beer to celebrate the return of HBO and MTV, Tyra reattached the foil and left for the library. He says he recycled the entire stunt two more times before his roomies and guests gave up on his TV set and left for another victim's place. Clearly a case of déjà view...

Tyra also passes along the information that clear fingernail polish applied liberally on the recording and playback heads of either an audio or video recorder will put an immediate stop to unwanted noise and confusion if certain uncaring people persist in annoying you with their cacophonic technology.

They call it simple and childish, but it made me laugh. And it works. They are Bryan S. and Rob M. and *it* is the simple stunt of getting back at nasty neighbors by standing outside their house or apartment and changing the channel selections on their TV sets using your own remote. You can really screw up and annoy their viewing, especially if you switch antenna sources on them. Most marks are too dumb to figure out what's happened. The mark might even call out a repair service.

See guys, it wasn't dumb, silly, or childish. Your TV stunt is fun, easy, and inexpensive. For us.

THERMOS

Squeamish had a work supervisor he didn't like because the guy bullied new workers and hassled the ladies without cause. The guy also worshiped for long periods each day at the shrine of St. Coffee. To this boss, drinking coffee all day beat working. Squeamish used that to beat him.

You take the jerk's coffee thermos and fill the attached cup with coffee, screw the filler plug back in, then put the full cup back on while holding the thermos upside down. After two days of getting doused, the jerk-mark finally turns his thermos upside down to open it. By this time, of course, you have removed the small plug from the main thermos body. Hot coffee goes everywhere.

THIEVES

I should dedicate this section to Sargento Smith, a truly wonderful law enforcement officer I knew in Panama. His answer to the question of thievery was simple and a lesson that could be well taken by all of us, regardless of race, creed, country of origin, political party, sexual preference, American or National League.

"Eet always work, mens," he told George, David, the Colonel, and me. "I shoot tievs...den dere no mo' problem."

I wonder if Sargento Smith is looking for work? Where was he when we needed an honest Attorney General in the late eighties? Speaking of real justice, Mad Man Mike and his pals, known as the Vengeful Angels of Justice, helped a friend who ran a small shop in one of the nastier neighborhoods of an Urban American Battlefield, i.e., a city.

"Some gang goon was shaking him down and he couldn't afford that. We learned what car the goon was driving and followed him to another location, where he was collecting from a business that sold dope to kids. While the goon was inside we smashed his car windshield and slashed his tires," Mike reports.

The same scenario was repeated two weeks later. Because they suspected the guy had a tail, they let him ride for a month. Then they followed him home and gave his car an acid bath and slashed the tires again.

"I heard he raised some hell with the bigger hoods on the turf, but he seemed to leave the little guys alone after that, guys like our pal," Mike added.

TIGHTWADS

Sometimes you get bitten by a mark with short arms and deep pockets. You know the type. The two or more of you go for snacks or beers and you always pay the tab. El cheapo, deadbeat, Number 10.

CD got back at one of these guys, a man who had deadbeat him for years, a cheap slob all the way. Being that both of them were basketball fans, CD fouled him that way.

"He knew I worked for a school district and asked me to get him a free or cheap basketball rim and hoop. The cheap bastard wouldn't buy one," CD told me.

"I found one we were going to pitch out. I took it to metal shop and changed the rim from the standard eighteen inches to sixteen inches. It was a perfectly finished job. I painted the rim orange and had a used net fastened on. It looked new and neat."

CD helped the cheapskate mark put up his "for-free" gift. CD then left so the mark could get acquainted with his new toy. CD told me that he has never looked back.

TIRES

When we need to bring the bad guys down, Ray Heffer is always there with a practical idea. He liked the old OSS tire spike idea, but found the store-bought variety a bit expensive. Ray made his own.

He uses 7D galvanized box nails. Cut off the heads and sharpen the blunt ends on your bench grinder. Now you have a long spike, sharp at both ends.

Cinch them in a bench vise and with a ball peen hammer bend them to form a right angle. Join two of the angles together, using an ordinary snap-spring clothespin to hold them together away from your vise while you solder the jointure.

As Ray says, "Remember when you played jacks as a kid? Remember that the jack always landed with a spike upward? So will your new, homemade tire spikes. Try it, you'll see."

By the way, Ray, please let me have your new, full address so I can get a proper thank-you to you.

TOILETS

I was going to refer to this section as Bathroom, but toilet is a much funnier word, according to B. Alice Anderson, agent for the BertGen comedy team so popular on the cable channels. Anyway, in some respects Americans are getting a bit more sophisticated about their toilet hygiene, in that bidets are now fairly common in newer housing and remodeling of bathrooms.

Funny story about bidets. When I was in the military service of my country, I was talking to a friend who had been stationed in Europe. Because of a severe housing shortage on base, his unit was temporarily housed in quarters formerly used for WAC personnel who were no longer on post. I asked him how he liked the WAC barracks.

"They were real fine, Sgt. Hayduke, except I didn't appreciate those squatty little water fountains you hadda get down on your hands and knees to get a drink," my friend related.

True story.

What the heck, it was a long time ago and the kid was from Mole Fart, Kentucky.

I can see all sorts of potential for using bidets to get back at your mark in minor ways, like adding soap, chemical additives, skin-coloring dyes, small critters, wasps, etc.

My Italian correspondent, Catzo Figa, has a wipeout of an idea involving toilet paper, aka bathroom stationery. Catzo says to impregnate your mark's TP with fiberglass, which can be done easily if you get the stuff in its amazingly fine powdery form.

The result is an itchy hassle you wouldn't wish on your, uhhh, worst mark. I would and so would Catzo. How can you go wrong?

You're in a public building. You walk by this door and see the nameplate logo on it, proclaiming GENTS in large letters. You think, "Wow, they have offices all over the world."

We've all been privileged to utilize the services of a pay toilet in our lives. Now, thanks to my wonderful sense of fun, we can utilize the services of a pay toilet to flush your mark right into a bad situation that he or she will have to take sitting down. It goes something like this...

Your mark goes into the stall, slips down his or her pants, slacks, skirt, or whatever. They are secured only around the mark's ankles. You stoop smartly down in front of the stall door and very quickly, briskly, and with great vigor, grab the skirt, pants, or whatever and yank them toward you as fast and hard as you can.

The immediate goal is to totally depants your mark. Hopefully, this will include the mark's underwear as well. You then leave the bathroom area, keeping the garments, giving them to some needy soul outside, or tossing them in the nearest waste receptacle.

Meanwhile, what of the mark, sitting there with no pants, skirt, underwear, etc.? Yes, what of the mark? I know I'm laughing already.

I found a poetess among my friends, when delectable Barby Buns told me that Thomas Carew once wrote that, "Love is the fart of every heart." Somehow I always thought that, ever since I've known Uncle Gerry and Rusty. Anyway, it seems this gossipy person was tattling about people all over the office, whether or not she knew any facts.

"She thought her ass was lily-white, of course, so we thought we'd reinforce that ego-image," Barby Buns told me. "We took some powdered limestone and spread it all over the toilet seat in her office john.

"After an hour's wait from her post-luncheon latrine visit, we noticed her scratching at her ass. She was gone back into the can for about ten minutes and we heard a lot of water running. When she came out her face was the only thing flushed. She took off the rest of the day."

Barby Buns said that the gossip slowed down a great deal after the Great Thunder Throne Whitewash Job.

Another simple additive to bathroom ambience was suggested by Bummer, who says you can spread chocolate cake icing, brown shoe polish, or other appropriate stain on toilet handles, bathroom doorknobs, light switches, etc. It's simple, but then so are the many marks who will fall for it.

While a college student, Pepper was dumped on by his school's financial aid people who wiped him out of some money due him by law.

"I felt that they'd nearly flushed my college career down the dumper, as I had to quit school for a year and work to make money to go back. When I did get back I became the Phantom Toilet Seat Adjuster," Pepper says. "It was easy. I'd unbolt the commode seats in the public restrooms but leave them in place. That way people would come in, sit down, and go crashing to the floor."

He says he was a unisex saboteur and that his work made headlines and letters to the editor in the school newspaper. His favorite hit was when one of the school's pompous vice presidents slid onto a urine-wetted floor and was so surprised that his bowels let loose on impact.

Sick Sid the Avenger had a problem with an employer whose responsibility included the public toilets in the building. Sid enjoyed low-intensity revenge warfare in the water closet. His plan was simple, quiet, and required few tools. Yet it was effective.

"I simply removed parts of the toilet mechanism without undue noise, tools, or complexity. Disconnect a few chains, a lever or two, unscrew the ball, purloin the plunger/water regulator," says Sick Sid.

"You have some laughs, because who looks inside the guts of the toilet tank before filling the bowl? You get the laughs and your mark gets the bill."

You will recall my suggestions for using carbide, the old miner's lamp fuel, instant fishing rod, etc.? CD has come through with another use that will add to the image of a fine, classy restaurant to which you owe a massive Haydukery. Or simply do this at work or school to enhance your own image among your peers.

Accompanied by your old pal carbide, go into the toilet stall. You may have already muttered something about having a huge load of digested chili, beans, eggs, or beer on board, and are so relieved to be relieving yourself of that load.

Inside the stall you are welcome to make appropriate sound effects, including bouncing your feet up and down, hitting the metal side of the stall, etc. When you're ready to leave, deposit some of the carbide into the toilet bowl, then toss in a lighted match. The mixture will burst into a bright but harmless flame, like a magician's trick. It will also make quite an odor.

CD says to be casual at this point, wash your hands, talk to colleagues, etc. Watch their reaction. Especially, he adds, note the reaction of the next guy slowly into and quickly out of that stall.

TOOL KIT

Grizzled is right. If you're going to do some serious Haydukery you need the proper tools. And while he and I work on a layperson's basic guide to the various tools, chemicals, natural products, etc., we've put together a basic kit of tools a beginner should have in his arsenal of Hayduking supplies. Here, then, is our basic kit.

- A 20-ounce straight claw hammer.
- A set of six screwdrivers, three slotted and three Phillips.
- An awl (a tool like an ice pick but with a heavier shaft).
- A large (12-inch) and a small (6-inch) crescent wrench.
- A set of pliers (including a channel lock, needle nose, and slip joint), and several wire cutters of differing sizes.
- A utility knife (aka razor blade knife), and an electrician's knife.
- A pry bar, preferably the flat kind.
- Several types of tape, including plastic electrical tape, duct tape, strapping tape, and masking tape.
- A glass cutter.

TOOTHPASTE

Don Silverman, the amusing talk show host from WJNO in South Florida, was on a camping trip with some friends, plus one other chap who was obnoxious, loud, and never quiet. He did his best to ruin the trip for Don and friends. Don felt it was time for the jerk to brush up on some courtesy.

In addition to being a motormouth, the jerk also ate more than his share of the food and never offered to help clean or cook. Don decided to toss an oral stinkbomb at this mark.

"One of the guys with a medical problem had a spare syringe. I made the next shopping run to the village for supplies and secretly bought some garlic oil," Don explained. "I loaded that syringe with garlic oil and carefully injected it into the boor's toothpaste."

For the rest of the camping experience, the mark complained bitterly about this lingering taste in his mouth. Meantime, his unwilling companions, who were using the guy's campsite, complained to him of his bad breath.

TOURISTS

We were in Zihuatanejo, a delightful Mexican town, and decided to play a bit of a prank on one of our companions, a rather reserved chap who was feeling some discomfort over being accosted by the aggressive little urchins of the street, i.e., kids wanting to sell us everything.

The man's son and I conspired to tell as many little kids as possible in a three block area, in faultless Spanish, of course, about this "rich, powerful American tourist" who was in the very streets of this town and how he was so very anxious to buy many American dollars worth of trinkets, clothes, bracelets, baskets, and the other flora of the Mexican street vendors.

We pointed him out to several children and referred to him as "El Señor Embajador" (Ambassador) and again related how rich and powerful he was. Our friend had no idea what we were saying about him until the siege of children began. Soon he was literally surrounded by a plague of shouting, selling children. He looked panicky. Adults began to gather, someone called a police officer. Our mark's son and I ducked into a convenient cantina around the corner to wait things out.

Our mark wasn't very happy about what we'd done when he at last spoke to us on the way back to our hotel. In true Hayduke fashion, we denied everything.

By the way, before any of you culture- or kiddy-sensitive souls gets on me for taking advantage of these Mexican kids, please let me educate you a bit. These kids have delightful senses of humor and laughed mightily about what had happened to our friend. Indeed, the next evening when his son and I were out walking, the same little kids came up to us laughing and asking us where was our friend, "El Gran Hombre" (the Big Man), and was "El Señor Embajador" coming to town, too.

UNIFORMS

Many marks wear white uniforms, e.g., cooks, navy personnel, hospital employees, lab technicians. Madman Mike advises that whites get really dirty very easily and very conspicuously. He adds that a sprinkling of graphite dust or sand, available from most auto supply shops and hardware stores, can make life conspicuous for your mark if sprinkled on a chair, seat, or wherever else s/he might park the old ass end.

"There are a lot of other ways to introduce this stuff to your mark's whites...I'll leave those details up to your readers, George," Mike adds.

One of my old military associates, a Brit named Sir Reggie Schmuck, OBE, PMS, AIDS, had a regular drill he pulled on deserving military marks. He usually found these bounders in one of the starch-laden units where correct form is more important than actual combat prowess.

"I'd wait until uniforms came from the cleaners and we all had delivery access. I would add a few unauthorized medals or ribbons to the mark's uniform, often from a foreign source, and preferably that of an enemy of the Queen, you know," Reggie related.

He said the stunt worked to order several times during receptions, reviews, and inspections where stuffy senior officers without humour pounced upon the hapless mark, who had never checked his own uniform blouse and had no idea what was on it.

U.S. POSTAL SERVICE

Every time we poor folks straighten up, the U.S. Postal Service, an odd misnomer, decides to play pick up the soap with us again. Two friends, Mr. Angry Consumer and Scifosa Maiale, have found a way to turn the USPS's cheek for a change. They suggest getting one of those preprinted, free postage, *For Official Business Only* envelopes from the clerk at a postal office window. It's easy. Buy a bunch of loose stamps and ask for an envelope to put them in.

Make sure no fingerprints go along as a hitchhiker on the envelope. Your next step is to carefully fill a cardboard carton with twenty or twenty-five pounds of something. Carefully seal it, then fasten that *For Official Business Only* envelope to it. You have already addressed that envelope to:

The Consumer Advocate
U.S. Postal Service
Washington DC 20260-6320

The guys suggest you might want to use the name and address of a secondary mark for the return address section of that envelope. Hey, all of that sure sounds like "official business" to me.

UTILITIES

Andrew McGeary tells us that in most states, natural gas companies are required by law to send a crew to your residence whenever you report a gas leak. You could send their repair crews to your mark's place at 3:00 or 4:00 on several cold, wet mornings to check the "overwhelming odor of escaping gas." You beg them not to call back to verify as "you," the mark, fear an explosion from static electricity when the phone rings. Sound hysterical when you call.

After a period of these pranks, introduce some butyl mercaptan into your mark's domicile. I have suggested the methodology in several other books, like through the ventilation system. Obviously the real fun starts when the mark actually does call in to report "another odd hour" gas leak.

The Wolf had a nasty co-worker who'd done some bad things to folks at work. He also lied and cheated on and about everything. Wolf decided to get him into deep feces with Mr. Electric Company. Here is Wolf's story.

Use a Bic lighter to melt off and undo the lead wire lock on the kw/h meter of your mark's home. Then, using lacing wire or liquid solder, put a halt to that numbered disc that rotates to indicate and record power usage. Reheat the lead tab and reseal the meter.

The deal is, according to Wolf, the mark will continue to receive and use power, but it will not be recording. When the meter reader comes to check the monthly use for billing purposes, the tampering will be obvious. The legal phrase here is Theft of Services.

If it's a first time deal and the mark has a clean rep, he'll probably not get into too much legal hassle. The power company will reset the meter and go away. Wait a month and repeat the trick. Wolf says to keep this up all year and maybe you'll get the mark canceled or, even better, fined and jailed.

UTILITY
COMPANIES

I first thought of this when I read a newspaper story about a midwestern power company. As justification for another rate rape, they cited the increase in line repair costs due to the proliferation of the small metallic balloons released by the thousands at mall openings, ball games, political rallies, and so forth. It seems the little buggers hit the high voltage transmission lines and cause outages.

My mind immediately conjured up various scenarios in which these little airborne boll weevils could be used deliberately. About six months later, I read in *EarthFirst!* that one of Pacific Gas & Electric's paid liars (aka a PR man) blamed these balloons for 140 power outages during 1987 in California alone. Southern California Edison reported 229 balloon-caused failures.

I also learned from the story that these balloons leave no trace because they usually disintegrate when they bust the power lines. Hmmmmmm. These little Mylar balloons have a one-thousandth of an inch coating of aluminum, a splendid conductor of electricity. When they hit lines, they either short the line or cause arcing between two lines. This usually melts lines and/or blows transformers. And these are just the little balloons. Can you imagine what larger versions might do?

Feud for thought, ain't it?

WEDDINGS

A sailor friend of mine referred to wedding bells as a storm warning, while Gary Hart once called his wedding ring a tourniquet—stopping his circulation. Weddings generally feature winners, losers, and personal acrimony. This is the stuff of pure Haydukery.

Thanks to such delightful friends as Hal Johnson, Dr. R. T. Scrotum, Ed Bluestone, and Penelope Penophile, I have compiled a shopping list of fun things you can choose to do at weddings, all of which are guaranteed to upset someone. The list follows:

1. Bring an inflatible sex doll to the ceremony as your date.

2. Get personal with it at the reception.

3. Make composite photos of either bride or groom showing him or her having sexual relations with a dog, child, or farm animal. Circulate these photos at the reception.

4. While moving through the reception line, spit on each person. Or hand each a condom and say, "Think about it!"

5. For a wedding present, give the bride a case of mouthwash, telling her loudly that it kills the gaggy taste of cum.

6. Beg someone's mother or grandmother to give you a hand job. You could tell her you have AIDS and don't want to pass it along.

7. Steal the cards from the wedding presents so nobody will know who gave what to whom.

8. Have a friend come to the church posing as a security

guard and demand to see each guest's invitation and identification.

9. Wear your underwear outside your clothing, especially if you are cross-dressing.

WINDOWS

Windows and glass doors belonging to your mark are always a fine target. Milk is a fine weapon with which to attack that target. My pal Andrei Zymurgy told me how he had to get back mildly at a friend who had tricked him. Andrei waited until January, when it is still very cold where he lives. He took several small balloons and filled them with canned milk, which is very sticky and thick.

He then launched his attack upon his friend's windows and sliding glass doors, plastering them with milk bombs. The stuff stuck to the cold glass and soon froze over in a milky, white film. Andrei says that the mark had to wait until late March until it grew warm enough to clean the windows. Until then, he had to do a lot of explaining to curious neighbors and visitors who asked about the ice-milked windows.

YELLOW PAGES

Do you have a nasty mark who is a also a prude, with his or her no's into everyone else's business? The Indiana Church Lady knew one of these jerks and conspired to have some fun by fingering the Yellow Pages. Here's how it happened.

"I used a local telephone directory to place an ad for my mark. I included some semi-erotic hints offering personal services, indicated 24-hour outcall services and acceptance of major credit cards. I named this business *Bobbi's Little Angels Of The Night* and listed my mark's home telephone number. The ad was placed under Escort Services and paid for in cash. It ran. So did my mark, for a new telephone number."

Church Lady says she did the exact same thing the following year in a neighboring town using the mark's new phone number.

YOUR MARK

A mark is really more than a bully or a deserved enemy or someone to whom you owe major revenge. A mark is also an easily recognized person who just demands to be revenged upon. Your mark is someone who pisses in your beer pitcher while you're being civilized in the restroom. Your mark is the kind of polyester pom-pom (aka lounge lizard) who walks up to a woman, leers, and says, "Hiya sex machine, what's your sign?" She, or you, looks back, right at its eyes and says, "Feces."

Your mark is the type of dipstick who goes for a Sunday drive so s/he can slow down to gawk at fresh car accidents, or the sort of creep who'd go to a stranger's funeral for an ego lift.

Remember, it really doesn't matter if whatever your mark fears above all else is really out there, as long as your mark really believes it is. In effect you become a fanged tortoise racing an unsuspecting or, perhaps, a very expecting paranoid hare.

Pay attention to your research and your intelligence-gathering. As people have pointed out, chances are if a mark has been nasty to you, he or she has done dirty to someone else, too. A slob is usually a slob, you might say.

Mr. Don't Know Him has some good advice for mark-dealing. He says to work your stunts so someone else breaks the shell around the ego of your mark, e.g., the local police, IRS, postal inspector, spouse, boss, or whomever.

ZYMURGY

Not only is this the last word listed in my dictionary, it also is the name given to the branch of chemistry of fermentation, i.e., brewing. I've been known to quaff a few cold ones from time to time. Anyway, my last words today are to ask you to please write to me and share your stunts, pranks, successes, or needs. I am always happy to hear from you and I do answer my own mail, all by myself. If you give me a return address when you write me, you'll hear from me. And, if your idea is new, funny, or nasty, it will probably appear in a future book.

I am:

George Hayduke
P.O. Box 1307
Boulder, CO 80306

Other books by George Hayduke:

GET EVEN
The Complete Book of Dirty Tricks

GET EVEN 2
More Dirty Tricks from the Master of Revenge

UP YOURS!
Guide to Advanced Revenge Techniques

MAKE 'EM PAY!
Ultimate Revenge Techniques from the Master
Trickster

SCREW UNTO OTHERS
Revenge Tactics for All Occasions

MAKE MY DAY!
Hayduke's Best Revenge Techniques for the Punks in
Your Life